THE LIFE RECOVERY®

WORKBOOK FOR

Grief

A Bible-Centered Approach for Taking Your Life Back

STEPHEN ARTERBURN
& DAVID STOOP

Tyndale House Publishers
Carol Stream, Illinois

Visit Tyndale online at liferecovery.com and www.tyndale.com.

TYNDALE, Tyndale's quill logo, and *Life Recovery* are registered trademarks of Tyndale House Publishers.

The Big Book is a registered trademark of A.A. World Services, Inc.

The Life Recovery Workbook for Grief: A Bible-Centered Approach for Taking Your Life Back

Copyright © 2020 by Stephen Arterburn and David Stoop. All rights reserved.

Cover photograph of purple abstract copyright © AVER/Depositphotos.com. All rights reserved.

Cover design by Dan Farrell

Edited by Ellen Richard Vosburg

The author is represented by the literary agency of Alive Literary Agency, 7680 Goddard Street, Suite 200, Colorado Springs, CO 80920, www.aliveliterary.com.

For information about special discounts for bulk purchases, please contact Tyndale House Publishers at csresponse@tyndale.com, or call 1-800-323-9400.

ISBN 978-1-4964-4213-0

Printed in the United States of America

26	25	24	23	22	21	20
7	6	5	4	3	2	1

This workbook is dedicated to every fellow struggler who has had the courage to face the truth about themselves, the humility to abandon their flawed attempts at living, and the willingness to find God's truth and live accordingly.

CONTENTS

The Twelve Steps of Alcoholics Anonymous

1. We admitted we were powerless over alcohol—that our lives had become unmanageable.
2. Came to believe that a Power greater than ourselves could restore us to sanity.
3. Made a decision to turn our will and our lives over to the care of God *as we understood Him.*
4. Made a searching and fearless moral inventory of ourselves.
5. Admitted to God, to ourselves, and to another human being the exact nature of our wrongs.
6. Were entirely ready to have God remove all these defects of character.
7. Humbly asked Him to remove our shortcomings.
8. Made a list of all persons we had harmed, and became willing to make amends to them all.
9. Made direct amends to such people wherever possible, except when to do so would injure them or others.
10. Continued to take personal inventory and when we were wrong promptly admitted it.
11. Sought through prayer and meditation to improve our conscious contact with God *as we understood Him*, praying only for knowledge of His will for us and the power to carry that out.
12. Having had a spiritual awakening as the result of these steps, we tried to carry this message to alcoholics, and to practice these principles in all our affairs.

The Twelve Steps

1. We admitted that we were powerless over our problems and that our lives had become unmanageable.
2. We came to believe that a Power greater than ourselves could restore us to sanity.
3. We made a decision to turn our wills and our lives over to the care of God.
4. We made a searching and fearless moral inventory of ourselves.
5. We admitted to God, to ourselves, and to another human being the exact nature of our wrongs.
6. We were entirely ready to have God remove these defects of character.
7. We humbly asked God to remove our shortcomings.
8. We made a list of all persons we had harmed and became willing to make amends to them all.
9. We made direct amends to such people wherever possible, except when to do so would injure them or others.
10. We continued to take personal inventory, and when we were wrong, promptly admitted it.
11. We sought through prayer and meditation to improve our conscious contact with God, praying only for knowledge of his will for us and the power to carry it out.
12. Having had a spiritual awakening as a result of these steps, we tried to carry this message to others, and to practice these principles in all our affairs.

The Twelve Steps used in *The Life Recovery Workbook* have been adapted with permission from the Twelve Steps of Alcoholics Anonymous.

INTRODUCTION

I am bent over and racked with pain. All day long I walk around filled with grief. (Psalm 38:6)

This workbook is about transformation from the death grip of grief to the restoration of life. It's about walking humbly, righteously, and mercifully with God while accepting his will. Often in our grief we oppose God, argue with him, plead with him for healing, and methodically cut other people out of our lives. We end up separated from God and from the people who care for us. We feel abandoned by all. The Twelve Steps are a path of finding that humble walk that leads us out of self-centered grief to acceptance and to a closer relationship with God.

We will be examining the Twelve Steps individually to consider the challenging spiritual lessons that allow us to move beyond our grief. Each step has a new task for us in our recovery from grief, but none of the steps stand alone. To effectively move through our grief to acceptance, we will work the steps in order. Each step prepares us for the next one, as we develop a greater sense of openness to God's plan and purpose in our lives.

We can get stuck in the grief process. But the path of recovery leads us through the grief process to a healthy acceptance of our loss. We see the Twelve Steps as a path and a process that makes us better disciples and more committed followers of Jesus Christ. Honesty, humility, and courage are vital components of faith that can move us beyond the grief of our losses back to a vibrant way of living as a follower of Jesus. Welcome to the journey.

STARTING AND LEADING A GROUP

Recovery is best experienced in the context of a group. Two or more willing people can form a powerful bond as they study and work these steps together. With little effort on your part, your struggles, problems, and hang-ups become a blessing to the group. As you open up, everyone else will feel more free to share from their own lives.

Being the leader of a group is actually quite simple. You can find many books on how to lead a small group, but here's a simple and effective way to do it:

1. Find a location in your home, a church, workplace, or school, and obtain permission (if necessary) to form the group.
2. Put up a few flyers announcing the time and place, calling it a grief support group, recovery group, or Twelve Step group.
3. Show up early, arrange the chairs, make some coffee, and welcome people as they arrive.
4. Start when you say you will start by opening in prayer and by reading the Twelve Steps and the correlating Scriptures.
5. Ask if anyone would like to share for three or four minutes. Don't allow others to "fix" the speaker, and if he or she goes on too long, be sure to enforce the time limit.
6. Make sure everyone has a copy of the workbook. Ask them to study Step One for discussion at the next meeting.
7. End when you say you will end by reading the Lord's Prayer.
8. Be sure that everyone knows where to get a workbook and a *Life Recovery Bible*, if they don't already have one.
9. E-mail Stephen Arterburn (Steve) at sarterburn@newlife.com, and tell him how it's going.
10. Feel good that you are allowing God to use you.

Please remember that working the steps is an art, not a formula. Most often, it is an individualized process.

God be with you on this journey. We pray that you will find healing, serenity, and peace of mind.

PROFILE

Sarah had a problem with anger. She had no idea where her anger came from. She just figured she was an angry person. But when she ruined her second computer by throwing it against the wall in anger, she realized she had a problem, and she didn't know what to do about it. Nothing she tried had reduced the intensity of her rage. She finally faced the reality that she needed someone to help her, so she made an appointment with a counselor.

Listening to Sarah's life story, the counselor took notice of the early death of Sarah's father and the relatively early death of her mother. When Sarah finished describing her background, the counselor returned to the subject of her parents' deaths. The counselor was particularly struck by the fact that whenever Sarah talked about her father, she would weep. But whenever she talked about her mother, she tried to hide the undercurrent of rage that she was experiencing.

Sarah's father had died when she was nine years old. He was her hero. He had lost one of his legs in the Korean War, but he had never let that slow him down. She was his little princess, and she was devastated when he died. But no one seemed to notice that Sarah was struggling with her emotions because all the adults were consumed by their own grief, especially her mother. So Sarah had to deal with the loss of her father on her own. She recalled how she would cry herself to sleep, night after night, for what felt like several years.

Her mother's response to her husband's death was to begin living her life through Sarah. Sarah was an only child, and everywhere her mother went, Sarah went with her. At first this was okay, but when Sarah became a teenager, she was often humiliated in front of her friends by how controlling her mother was. Even when they went to church, Sarah was forced to sit with her mother, whereas all the other teenage girls sat as a group. Sarah begged and pleaded with her mother to let her sit with her friends in church and to spend time with her friends during the week, but Sarah's mother always responded with sadness and tears. Soon Sarah's begging and pleading turned into yelling and screaming. When Sarah was twenty-five, her mother died. Sarah felt relieved and had to force herself to go to the funeral.

Her counselor understood that complete grieving involves the experience of both anger as a protest and sadness as a sense of resignation. Acceptance of the loss is the final stage of grieving. The counselor realized that Sarah was experiencing incomplete grieving in relation to the deaths of both her father and her mother. In relationship to her father, she experienced only sadness. In response to her mother's death, she experienced only anger as a protest.

So the counselor began to talk to Sarah about things that she had missed due to her father's early death. When the counselor hit on the fact that, due to her father's early death, she was exposed to her mother's smothering behavior, it rang a bell in Sarah. If her dad had lived, she'd have had a very different relationship with her mother. Gradually Sarah began to see her father's death as both sad and something to protest with anger.

In the same way, the counselor began to challenge her to see her mother as being weak and needy and unable to acknowledge her own problems. Sarah began to feel a sense of sadness for what she had lost in her relationship with her mother. Eventually, Sarah was able to feel some anger as protest over the incredible loss of her father at such a young age and to feel some sadness at the limitations she experienced in her relationship with her mother.

It took some time for Sarah to complete the grieving process for each of her parents. But along the way, she noticed that she was not as troubled by the out-of-control anger that she had experienced previously, which led her to get into counseling. Now, ten years later, Sarah hasn't ruined a single computer. In fact, she very seldomly gets angry, and she can talk about her father without crying. She can also talk about her mother without getting angry. She worked through the process of grieving to reach acceptance. Sarah was powerless to solve the issue by herself, but she wisely chose to get help, and God worked through her counselor to help Sarah get beyond her powerlessness.

STEP ONE

We admitted we were powerless over our problems and that our lives had become unmanageable.

It's interesting that the first word in the first step is *we.* I can't work on my problems in my life on my own. The resolution comes through the *we.* One of the things Sarah had done over the years was to increasingly isolate herself from relationships with other people in order to hide her rage. Then, if her rage suddenly got out of control, no one would be around to see it. She was powerless, but she was not helpless. So she got help. The Twelve Steps teach us that recovery and healing always take place in the context of the *we.*

Spiritual transformation always begins in community. At the start of Jesus' ministry, he began to gather people around him as his disciples. The power of the early church in the book of Acts is directly related to their reputation for how they loved one another. So even grieving needs to take place in some sort of community, whether that community is an official grief support group or simply a family gathering around each other and staying connected as they grieve.

The key point of Step One is the reality of our powerlessness. It's not a term we like. In fact, it's an experience that we seek to avoid as much as possible. But when it comes to grieving over our losses, we are all too often confronted with the reality of our powerlessness to do anything about what has been lost. When we have lost someone or something important, especially a loved one, we are truly powerless.

We can even experience powerlessness when we lose something that seems small. One time, I (Dave) lost a treasured old fountain pen in a restaurant. But no matter how many times I went back to the restaurant to look for it, it was gone. I was powerless to do anything about it. I even offered a reward for its return. I talked to the waiters and waitresses. But no matter what I did, I was confronted with the fact that I had no power. I was powerless.

When someone I love is lying in a hospital bed on the verge of death, no matter how much I plead with the doctors or how much I pray, I am confronted with my own powerlessness in the face of loss. In those circumstances, even the doctors often acknowledge their powerlessness to do anything to avoid the inevitable. So the first step of grieving is to come to terms with our powerlessness.

Some of our losses are obvious: I lost my fountain pen; I lost my friend to cancer. But there are other losses that are not so obvious. For example, I lost my image of myself when I lost my fountain pen because I thought I was so careful with that pen. I lost a sense of connection when my friend died and left me here without him. When my children grew up and moved out of our house, I lost the sense of connection we had when we lived under the same roof. When we moved across the country,

I lost a sense of familiarity with where I lived, and I lost a circle of friends.

When we look at how people grieved in the Bible, they had certain rituals and behaviors that they followed. Perhaps that mitigated some of the powerlessness they were feeling. For example, when someone died, those who were mourning tore their clothes and put on burlap. Sometimes they shaved their heads or they threw ashes on themselves. It's almost as if they felt like they had to do something in the midst of their grief to avoid the feeling of powerlessness.

The account of Job's suffering teaches us some important things about grief. When Job received word that all of his animals were gone, that his sons and daughters were all dead, that all his sheep and the shepherds were gone, that all his camels were gone, and that almost all of his servants were killed, the Bible says that Job "stood up and tore his robe in grief. Then he shaved his head and fell to the ground to worship" (Job 1:20). Job responded, "I came naked from my mother's womb, and I will be naked when I leave. The LORD gave me what I had, and the LORD has taken it away. Praise the name of the LORD!" (Job 1:21). It's interesting that in his grief Job also worshiped—he stayed connected to God.

Job had to acknowledge his powerlessness because everything had already happened by the time he heard, and there was nothing he could do. All his cattle were gone, his servants were gone, all his children were gone, and all his wealth was gone. There was nothing he could do about any of it!

But he had friends, and three of them came to comfort and console him. He wasn't going to be alone. The three friends sat in silence with him, which was the perfect response. When you're grieving, you don't want a lot of conversation. The passage says, "They sat on the ground with him for seven days and nights. No one said a word to Job, for they saw that his suffering was too great for words" (Job 2:13). Then Job spoke, and the silence was broken.

Then Job was angry. When he spoke, he first cursed the day of his birth. He wished he had never been born. From the sadness of chapters 1 and 2 to the anger of chapter 3, Job has been grieving. And Job's friends are going to make him even more angry. At one point, Job says to them, "How long will you torture me? How long will you try to crush me with your words? You have already insulted me ten times. You should be ashamed of treating me so badly" (Job 19:2-3). The friends meant well, but their responses didn't comfort Job.

Job was protesting his innocence, and he directed his arguments at God. And finally, when God begins to respond to Job, he doesn't criticize Job for arguing. Instead, God asks Job a series of questions that cover four chapters—questions Job cannot answer, for the questions are too profound. We cannot answer some of these questions to this day. God confronted Job with his powerlessness. When God is finished, Job says,

> "I know that you can do anything, and no one can stop you. You asked, 'Who is this that questions my wisdom with such ignorance?' It is I—and I was talking about things I knew nothing about, things far too wonderful for me. You said, 'Listen and I will speak! I have some questions for you, and you must answer them.' *I had only heard about you before, but now I have seen you with my own eyes.* I take back everything I said, and I sit in dust and ashes to show my repentance." (Job 42:1-6, emphasis added).

What is it that Job learned from his powerlessness? For one, even though he was powerless, he was talking to a very powerful God. And he repented for having too small an image of God. That's something we can learn from Job. When we are truly powerless, we are open to the almighty power of God himself. There's no sense by which I can do it myself: I can do it only with God's help.

But is it okay to argue with God? God says it is. He told Job to go pray for his friends because they did not speak rightly about him. But Job was not corrected or criticized for all of his arguing with God! So Job teaches us that it's okay to argue with God as long as we remember that we are arguing with a very big, powerful God.

One more important thing about powerlessness we learn from Jesus. In his ministry he highlighted the importance of children. At one point, some little children tried to come and visit Jesus, but his disciples tried to turn them away. Jesus stopped his disciples and said, "Let the children come to me. Don't stop them! For the Kingdom of Heaven belongs to those who are like these children" (Matthew 19:14). The Kingdom of Heaven belongs to the little children who were basically powerless.

We sometimes think that being powerless is like being a victim. It doesn't make us a victim: It really just gets us out of the way for God to work. One of the major tasks in our grieving is to come to terms with our powerlessness, for we are truly powerless when we are dealing with our losses. But remember, like Sarah and Job, we are not helpless.

QUESTIONS FOR **STEP ONE**

Trapped Genesis 16:1-15

1. How is my experience of powerlessness similar to Hagar's experience? How is it different?

_____

_____

_____

_____

2. How have I tried to escape from the pain of my grief?

_____

_____

_____

_____

_____

3. What has been my experience of anger in my grief? What scares me about my anger?

_____

_____

_____

_____

_____

4. How have I experienced sadness in my grief? What scares me about my sadness?

_____

_____

_____

_____

_____

5. What are some of my fears about grieving this loss?

_____

_____

_____

_____

6. Where can I see God in this process of grieving right now?

_____

_____

_____

_____

_____

The Fruit of Grieving _Genesis 41:50-52_

1. Due to the jealousy and hatred of his brothers, Joseph was sold into slavery and ended up in Egypt. He managed to excel in serving his master, but his master's wife accused him of attempted rape. He spent several years in prison, until he was finally released by Pharaoh. He became the second most powerful man in Egypt, and when he had children, he gave them meaningful names. Joseph named his second son Ephraim, which sounds like a Hebrew word meaning "fruit-ful," because he said "God has made me fruitful in this land of my grief" (Genesis 41:52). What was Joseph's fruitfulness in Egypt, the land of his grief?

_____

_____

_____

_____

2. What are some ways I can see God producing fruit in my life in the midst of my grief?

_____

_____

_____

_____

All Is Darkness *Job 6:2-13*

1. Job is very clear about the pain he was feeling. Describe the pain you're experiencing in your grieving.

_____

_____

_____

2. In what ways have I felt totally powerless in my grief?

_____

_____

_____

3. In what ways have I tried to be faithful to God in the midst of my pain?

_____

_____

_____

4. How has Job's experience helped me in experiencing my grief?

_____

_____

_____

Worn Out from Sobbing *Psalm 6:1-10*

1. How does my sadness affect my relationships?

_____

_____

_____

2. In what ways have others misunderstood my grief?

_____

_____

_____

3. David seems to project his anger onto God. That's why we need to get comfortable expressing our anger in relationships, especially in our relationship with God. Remember, anger is a protest. In what ways have I brought my protest into relationship?

_____

_____

_____

4. Who in my circle of friends would be able to help me restore my confidence in God?

_____

_____

_____

Like Little Children _Mark 10:13-16_

1. When I feel powerless, do I feel like a little child? How does that feel?

_____

_____

_____

2. When do I feel most cared for?

_____

_____

_____

3. How does being childlike help me depend on God?

_____

_____

_____

The Paradox of Powerlessness _2 Corinthians 4:7-10_

1. Remember some examples of when you have accepted your
   own powerlessness and embraced God's powerfulness.
   Describe them in this space below.

_____

_____

_____

2. How do I respond to trouble?

_____

_____

_____

3. How do I respond to being perplexed?

_____

_____

_____

4. What do I do when it feels like God has abandoned me?

_____

_____

_____

_There is great power in realizing
that we are powerless._

PROFILE

Andy was sitting in the counselor's office talking about the house fire that destroyed everything his family owned. The fire was almost fifty years ago. He was twelve years old at the time. He recalled the setting: His dad was in the garage, working on the family car. Andy and his mom were sitting on the porch. Mom was reading a book, and he was working on finishing a model airplane. His two sisters were at a friend's house. It was a perfect afternoon on a lazy summer day. Even the dog was contently resting in the doorway.

Suddenly there was an explosion, and the whole house seemed to be engulfed in flames at once. His dad barely escaped from the garage, and he and his mother ran from the porch to safety. Later they noticed, the dog was missing some of her whiskers that were apparently a casualty of the flames.

When the firemen finally left, the family stood in shocked silence. They were so grateful for simply being alive, but they soon realized that everything they owned had been destroyed. They were left with only the clothes on their backs—literally.

It didn't take long for their pastor and his wife to pull up to the disastrous scene. They told Andy's family that they were going to come and live with the pastor and his wife until they got resettled. People from their church brought boxes of clothing for them to choose from. Someone loaned them a car. Their church family gathered around Andy's family and provided the support and resources they needed.

Andy related to his counselor that the sadness was easy to experience. He was sad to lose his collection of model airplanes that he had built, along with some other keepsake items he had collected. The family talked about things they had lost and the sadness of losing them. Andy couldn't recall that there was ever any protest or anger over their losses. They were just too grateful to be alive. But as Andy talked to the counselor, he recalled he and his two sisters frequently expressed their anger at God; they were even angry at their dad, blaming him for what had happened.

An interesting comment from Andy is that in the forty years that have passed since the fire, he has never worked on his own car—he's always used a mechanic. Perhaps that was the one residual from the losses of that fateful day. But there was always the memory of the incredible outpouring of support the family got from the pastor and his wife and from their church family. Andy and his family were certainly powerless during that period of life, but they were just as certainly not helpless.

STEP TWO

We came to believe that a Power greater than ourselves could restore us to sanity.

When Andy's family lost their home and all their earthly belongings, they were forced to face their powerlessness. They could do nothing about the situation. It was a season of insanity, in part, because it had happened so suddenly. There was nothing anyone could do. But when the pastor and his wife invited the family to stay with them, it was like a Power greater than themselves was available to them. Their pastor represented a Power that was greater than the insanity. The pastor and his family represented the community of believers and the person of Jesus Christ.

This step tells us what to do as soon as possible when life throws us a curve. But we typically don't listen because our tendency is to deal with the situation on our own terms. We try to deny the reality of our powerlessness by developing coping skills. But instead of solving our problems, we multiply them. Insanity is sometimes defined as doing the same thing over and over again, expecting different results.

Andy and his family were challenged to live out the reality that both Paul and James affirm in Scripture. Paul says, "We can rejoice, too, when we run into problems and trials (Romans 5:3)." James says, "When troubles of any kind come your way, consider it an opportunity for great joy" (James 1:2). Both Paul and James explain that when our faith is being tested, our endurance in the faith has a chance to grow. Paul adds that "endurance develops strength of character, and character strengthens our confident hope of salvation. And this hope will not lead to disappointment" (Romans 5:4-5).

It takes character to acknowledge that we are powerless, and we need to seek the help of someone who is more powerful than we are. Otherwise we just perpetuate the insanity. In our self-sufficiency, we think God is being unfair or is somehow against us. Job demonstrated this tendency as he argued with God and protested his innocence. It wasn't until God started asking him questions that Job understood how powerless he was and how his protestations only led to more insanity.

David describes this kind of insanity in several of his psalms. In Psalm 31:10, he says, "I am dying from grief; my years are shortened by sadness. Sin has drained my strength; I am wasting away from within." And in Psalm 38:6, he says, "I am bent over and racked with pain. All day long I walk around filled with grief." The prophet Isaiah says, "My heart is heavy with grief. Weep for me, for I wither away" (Isaiah 24:16).

When our hearts and minds are swirling around in the depths of our grief, we need to find someone more powerful than ourselves to walk the journey with us. Who is more powerful than Jesus?

Picture the scene in Matthew 8:23-27. Jesus got into a boat with his disciples and quickly fell asleep in the back of the boat. He seemed oblivious to the massive waves in the storm that they encountered. Several of his disciples lived on that lake when they worked as fishermen. But this was a storm like none they had ever encountered before. The waves were so big that the disciples, including the fishermen, were terrified. But Jesus continued sleeping.

In their fear and desperation, they woke Jesus with these words, "Lord, save us! We're going to drown!" (Matthew 8:25). Jesus answered them, "'Why are you afraid? You have so little faith!' Then he got up and rebuked the wind and waves, and suddenly there was a great calm" (Matthew 8:26). The waves that had been engulfing the boat suddenly stopped, and the sea was like glass. The wind that had been threatening to sink the boat suddenly stopped. And in that great calm, the disciples in amazement said, "Who is this man? . . . Even the winds and waves obey him!" (Matthew 8:27). That's power! And he wants to be our Higher Power, for he is the highest power.

We simply need to have the same attitude as the woman who was suffering from constant bleeding. She had tried everything, and nothing had worked. She saw Jesus in the crowd and thought, "If I can just touch his robe, I will be healed" (Mark 5:28). She is an example of our need to reach out right now, not just to our brothers and sisters in the Lord, but to the Lord Jesus himself. Now.

Coming to believe in Step Two is a process of our becoming aware of a greater reality than anything we can see with our eyes. God is willing, at any moment, to join with us in our grief and in our painful emotions. By engaging in this process, we allow God to move us through the grief process and to strengthen our ability to have faith in his power.

QUESTIONS FOR **STEP TWO**

Honest Grieving *1 Samuel 1:1-18*

1. What are some ways my grief has been misunderstood by others?

_____

_____

_____

_____

2. How have I tried to hide my feelings of grief?

_____

_____

_____

_____

3. Who has been the "Eli" in misunderstanding my grief?

_____

_____

_____

_____

4. Who has understood the pain of my heart? How has that person helped me in working through my grief?

_____

_____

_____

_____

Internal Bondage *Mark 5:1-13*

1. What self-destructive behaviors have I been tempted to do? List and describe them.

_____

_____

_____

_____

2. How has my grief kept me from living in the present? In what ways have I been more comfortable living in tombs of isolation and silent judgment?

_____

_____

_____

_____

3. What motivated me to *come to believe* that I needed to rely on Jesus?

_____

_____

_____

_____

Healing Faith *Luke 8:43-48*

1. How have I tried to grieve in my own power?

_____

_____

_____

_____

2. What other ways have I thought about grieving in my own power? What were the results?

_____

_____

_____

3. Am I ready to reach out to Jesus as my Higher Power? Write a note to God about your readiness.

_____

_____

_____

Believe _Romans 1:18-20_

1. What experiences in my life have shown me that self-sufficiency is unsustainable?

_____

_____

_____

2. How have I seen God's power at work in other people's lives?

_____

_____

_____

3. What are some signs that I am on the path to being restored to sanity?

_____

_____

_____

Rejoice Always *Romans 5:3-11; James 1:2-4*

1. How do I think powerlessness relates to my ability to rejoice in the midst of my troubles?

_____

_____

_____

2. When I accept my powerlessness and I am able to rejoice in the midst of my pain, what do Paul and James say will be the result?

_____

_____

_____

Hope in Faith *Hebrews 11:1-10*

1. Am I able to believe that God can help me to live through my grief? How can I live out my trust that God will help?

_____

_____

_____

2. Can I now believe that, as I reach out for God and surrender to him, he will be present and ready to help? Why or why not?

_____

_____

_____

Faith begins when we believe
that God is who he says he is.

PROFILE

C. S. Lewis's book *A Grief Observed* is his reflection on the process of grieving for his wife, Joy Davidman, who was diagnosed with cancer soon after they were married. It is based on a journal he kept in the months following her passing. The book is very clear about his anger with God. He struggled with his faith, especially during the early days of his journey through the different stages of grieving.

In the beginning of the book, he holds back on none of his questioning of God, even his goodness. Lewis questions things he had held as certainties prior to her illness and death. His wife's death also reminded him that his mother had died of cancer when he was a young boy and that his father had died of cancer as well. Davidman's death brought back the feelings of grief he felt over his parents' deaths.

Lewis recounts how he struggled with his inability to feel his emotions at times. But he also scolds himself for his "maudlin tears." The most helpful part of the book is his honesty about his struggle with the nature and character of God. He feared losing his faith because the grief was so intense. Lewis remarks about how he was tempted to believe untruths about God, such as God doesn't really care for us, he can hurt us intentionally, and he is conspicuously absent when our need is most severe. This was part of his struggle in the early stages of his grief.

In the end he realizes that his belief in God had not so much been in God for who he is but in the hopeful ideas of his own construction. Lewis's conclusion is much like Job's when he responds after his encounter with God: "I had only heard about you before, but now I have seen you with my own eyes. I take back everything I said, and I sit in dust and ashes to show my repentance" (Job 42:5-6).

Later in the grieving process, as his anger receded, Lewis's memory of his wife begins to emerge out of his grief. He can see both his wife and God more clearly and more accurately. He comes to a point where he understands that one of God's intentions in the loss of a spouse is that it is an expected and necessary next step in this life. God also uses loss and pain in our lives to teach us to know and trust him as he is, rather than as we would like him to be. Lewis believed that before his wife's illness, and he was able to recapture it as he moved through his grieving process.

The lesson is that, like Job, we can argue with God in our grief, we can question God's motives, and we can even question deeply held truths about God and his nature, for God understands what it is to grieve. God is more concerned that we learn to trust him through the grieving process than with the questions we have in the midst of the process.

STEP THREE
We made a decision to turn our wills and our lives over to the care of God.

In Step Three we decide to turn our wills, our ways, and our entire lives over to God. That includes all our losses. It sounds like a simple task. After all, we have probably turned our lives over to Christ at some point before. But this goes beyond salvation. Now we intentionally release our hopes, dreams, choices, relationships, and losses, giving God control over all of it. It is not just a onetime commitment, as we certainly will learn. It's meant to be a way of life.

This step challenges us to trust God on a deeper level than ever before. Everything we have experienced up to this point may make us somewhat skeptical and wary, especially when we are called to trust God completely with our losses. Here we are called to give up our self-sufficiency. It's no longer theoretical; it's real. After all, none of the people we can see and touch have proven to be trustworthy. This of course leads us to struggle in our ability to trust God, whom we cannot see.

Confronting our lack of trust in God's care is critical in working the rest of the Twelve Steps. For us to move through the grieving process, we must learn to completely surrender not only ourselves, but especially our wills. That's the hard part: surrendering our wills. As Jesus said, "If you give up your life for me, you will find it" (Matthew 10:39).

This is not only a battle of the wills—God's will vs. my will—but also a spiritual battle. But once again we go back to the whole powerlessness situation where we think we have control—but we really don't. We must face the fact that we live with an illusion of control. Only God has ultimate control. Once we accept this, then our dependence on him helps us move through the grieving process. And he grieves with us, for he cares deeply for each of us.

What Step Three asserts is that we are choosing to draw closer to God in the midst of our grieving. God understands grief. Isaiah describes the future Messiah by saying, "He was despised and rejected—a man of sorrows, acquainted with deepest grief" (Isaiah 53:3). So that's why we say God grieves with us. Through his own experience of suffering, he understands our need to grieve.

In Step One, we admitted that we do not have power over anything in our lives. In Step Two, we acknowledged that God does have power to work in our lives, especially as we grieve. Now in Step Three, we decide to turn everything over to him, let go, and ask for his help. These are acts of humility that allow God's Spirit to draw us close. When our own wills are out of the way, God can work in our hearts. We may not see immediate results, but in turning our whole selves over to the care of God, we exchange our heavy burdens for the rest and peace that Jesus brings.

As we choose to give our wills, our thoughts, our decisions, our grief, and our behaviors "to the care of God," we rest in the belief that he cares for us. He is with us no matter what life throws at us. With his power and his presence, we are able to effectively move through the grieving process without getting bogged down in depression or hopelessness. Step Three is the foundation for the subsequent actions we will take as we work the remainder of the Twelve Steps.

QUESTIONS FOR **STEP THREE**

Trusting God *Numbers 23:18-24*

1. What in my life has led me to mistrust God?

_____

_____

_____

_____

_____

2. What have I done to cause others not to trust me?

_____

_____

_____

_____

_____

3. What keeps me from surrendering to God?

_____

_____

_____

_____

It's Your Choice _Deuteronomy 30:15-20_

1. What is it about my understanding of God that prevents
   me from deciding to turn my life and my will over to his
   care?

_____

_____

_____

_____

2. How does fear affect my choices?

_____

_____

_____

_____

Giving Up Control _Psalm 61:1-8_

1. Where did I get the illusion that I can control other people
   or my circumstances, job, or life?

_____

_____

_____

_____

2. What stops me from surrendering my will and my life so that I can find the life God intends for me?

_____

_____

_____

_____

_____

_____

Redeeming the Past _Isaiah 54:4-8_

1. How do I hold God at arm's length? Why?

_____

_____

_____

_____

2. What fears have the most power in my life?

_____

_____

_____

_____

3. How is shame connected to my fears?

_____

_____

_____

_____

God Is Faithful *Lamentations 3:16-27*

1. What about my circumstances now makes it hard for me to believe that God is faithful?

_____

_____

_____

_____

2. What crushed hopes and dreams am I grieving right now?

_____

_____

_____

_____

3. As Jeremiah grieves over fallen Jerusalem in this passage, he reminds himself of God's faithfulness. What can I call to mind that reminds me of God's faithfulness?

_____

_____

_____

_____

Discovering God *Acts 17:22-28*

1. How do I define the word *surrender*?

_____

_____

_____

_____

2. What is the difference between *my will* and *my life*?

_____

_____

_____

_____

When what we believe, say, and do all line up,
we can have enough faith to turn everything over to God.
But this alignment happens only when we have enough faith
to turn everything over to God—every compartment, every
hidden secret, everything—and acknowledge, perhaps for the
very first time, that God is the Higher Power in our lives.

PROFILE

Fred had been retired two years when he and his wife, Melissa, took the trip of their dreams. They were gone for two months. In their travels they visited several underdeveloped countries, and they even visited one of the children they had supported over the years in an African country. Towards the end of the trip, Melissa started to complain about not feeling well. They made an appointment with her doctor as soon as they returned home.

The doctor ran several tests that were inconclusive, and he told her that it would probably pass and she shouldn't worry about it. But he wanted her to keep him posted. When the symptoms persisted, she made another appointment with him, and after several more tests, he referred her to a specialist in infectious diseases. The doctor admitted that he had never run into the kind of symptoms she was having.

The specialist was puzzled as well. She ran a different series of tests, but they also revealed nothing new. All the while, Melissa kept growing sicker and sicker and weaker and weaker. Even after two hospitalizations and a whole battery of different tests, they couldn't put a name to what she was experiencing. It was apparently some strange bug she had picked up somewhere in their travels.

As Melissa grew weaker, she spent all of her time either on the couch, in the bed, or in the bathroom. Fred became the cook and bottle washer, and he said he was just grateful that this was happening after he retired. He stayed busy taking care of all of Melissa's physical needs as best he could. But Melissa kept going downhill physically, even though her mind was as sharp as ever.

Finally the day came that Fred had to move Melissa into an assisted care facility. Every day Fred visited her in the morning and secretly brought Melissa her favorite lunch. He took a break to get his own lunch, but then he spent most of the afternoon with her as well. He never missed a day.

Melissa stayed sharp mentally to the end. It was five years from the day Melissa started feeling sick to the day she died. Fred said over that period of time he certainly learned what power-lessness is all about. They felt fortunate that they already had a relationship with the highest power, Jesus. They had willingly turned their wills and their lives over to the care of God.

That didn't mean there were not times of great frustration, especially when they couldn't get a diagnosis or even answers to their questions. There were many times they argued with God, but that always led to more prayer time together. Gradually there was a growing acceptance, not only of what was going on with Melissa but also of all the changes that were required. Today Fred talks about the incredible lessons he learned about himself and about his relationship with God through that terrible time. It was definitely a time of character building for Fred.

Not too long after Melissa died, a friend who was in his own recovery suggested that Fred do an inventory of his life now that Melissa was gone. Fred told him that he felt like there was a great void in his life. His friend replied, "Now might be the time for you to take an inventory of what your 'new normal you' is going to look like."

STEP FOUR

We made a searching and fearless moral inventory of ourselves.

To this point in the Twelve Steps, the work we have done has been related to our thought processes, attitudes, and beliefs. We have moved out of the area of denial into the reality of our grieving. We have admitted that we are powerless and have come to believe that only God can and will walk with us through this process. We have surrendered our lives and our wills to the care of God. In other words, we have chosen to "let go and let God." Now that that decision has been made, it's time for action.

Like Fred, we're going to look at two kinds of inventory. One inventory will be a searching and fearless inventory that we need to take of ourselves in order to examine who we are. This is of immense value in getting to know ourselves. We also suggest that you do an inventory of the "new normal you" that is growing with the loss of your loved one or with the loss of something else significant, like a job. The "new normal you" inventory will be an attempt to define what your life is going to be like in the future. The searching and fearless moral inventory looks back at what your life has been up to this point. So get ready.

It is a fearful and heartbreaking exercise to face our own brokenness. It is easy to stop the recovery process at this step simply by delaying getting started. That's why it's a fearless inventory, for we begin to look at ourselves at a deeper level.

Step Four is designed to answer the question "Who am I?" But in working the steps through our grieving process, the question also becomes "Who am I now?" Not only did we lose someone or something very important to us, we have also lost the definition of who we are. We need to learn about how we operate in this world without whoever or whatever we are grieving.

Early in the history of the Twelve Step program, people began their inventories by looking at how they measured up to the Four Absolutes: *honesty, purity, unselfishness,* and *love.* These are positive absolutes, but they are absolutes that everyone fails to meet at some point. So our searching and fearless inventories would include our failures to be honest, our failures to be sexually and morally pure, our failures to be unselfish, and our failures to love. The "new normal you" inventory is the process by which we find new ways of managing life in the midst of new circumstances. Some people try to survive in the tangle of emotions they are experiencing, and that is a very normal and common reaction, but we want to get beyond just coping.

When you begin your inventories, think of how a business takes inventory by counting their supplies or merchandise. Taking an inventory tells a business what amount is adequate, what is surplus, what is useless, and what might be a liability. When we take the "new normal you" inventory, we look at how what we have lost affects our everyday lives. For example, if we lost a loved one with whom we made decisions together, we will have to learn a different way to make decisions. Previously, we had someone to discuss the choices with, but now we have to learn to make those decisions on our own. We have to take stock of what our lives are like now, compare it with what our lives were like before, and redefine ourselves and our behaviors accordingly. We must examine our lives spiritually, emotionally, physically, and socially. We will need to describe an authentic, "new normal you" self in every aspect of our lives.

Our "new normal you" inventories must also be fearless. The purpose of taking inventory of our lives is to help us face the truth about ourselves. Truth is the opposite of denial. By putting the truth in writing, we determine that we are ready to break free from the patterns and behaviors of denial.

We also know that facing the truth will be painful because we are also facing the reality of everything we have lost over the course of our lives. It's never easy to look at our abuses, shame, and disappointments. Even though this is a time of discomfort, we know that the steps of recovery can lead us to humility and to a life full of happiness. It may not feel that way as we work on our inventories, but those who have made the journey before us will testify to that truth.

When Jesus came to earth, he brought with him "grace and

truth" (John 1:14, KJV). Here's how the New Living Translation puts it: "So the Word [Jesus] became human and made his home among us. He was full of unfailing love and faithfulness." This step is a process of facing the truth with God's help. When we face the truth, we will also experience God's grace, his unfailing love. The more we experience the truth, the more we will experience God's grace. If we allow God's grace to change us, then we will develop an attitude of humility and have a teachable heart. We will feel accepted for who we are by the God who created us.

We also need to be careful as we inventory our lives. Our prideful, old sin nature can cause us to forget the journey of the first three steps, and we will return to our self-centered ways of thinking and behaving. So we need to approach our inventories with humility, not pride. We demonstrate pride when we hold on to resentments, when we are motivated by fear, and when we are dishonest about our moral or sexual misconduct. Pride will keep us from knowing God's will and feeling his presence as we seek to define what our "new normal you" life is going to be.

The good news about this work is that we will gain an honest picture of ourselves as we face the "new normal you." Letting go of resentments and fears by working the first three steps has prepared us to define ourselves as authentic followers of Jesus Christ. Serenity and peace of mind will flow into our lives as a result of surrendering our wills and our lives to God.

QUESTIONS FOR **STEP FOUR**

Coming Out of Hiding Genesis 3:6-13

1. When we are in the process of grieving, we tend to isolate ourselves from others so that we can hide our pain and

suffering. We hide because we feel ashamed. In what ways have I been hiding?

_____

_____

_____

_____

2. How has shame taken root in my heart? What are some of the results that I've experienced from feeling ashamed of my grief?

_____

_____

_____

_____

3. What holds me back from trying to be more open with those I trust?

_____

_____

_____

_____

Enter into the Sadness _Nehemiah 8:7-10_

1. What painful memories keep me from writing my searching and fearless inventory or my "new normal you" inventory? Describe them here.

_____

_____

_____

_____

2. What painful memories am I afraid of facing?

_____

_____

_____

_____

3. What role has shame from past mistakes played in keeping me from starting and completing an inventory?

_____

_____

_____

_____

4. Is my pride keeping me from starting my inventory?

_____

_____

_____

_____

_____

Confession _Nehemiah 9:1-3_

1. What behaviors over my lifetime have been offensive to God?

_____

_____

_____

_____

2. What bad habits do I need to identify in my life and confess to God?

_____

_____

_____

_____

3. Why am I still resistant to being honest with God?

_____

_____

_____

_____

4. What consequences from past wrong choices am I living with today?

_____

_____

_____

_____

It's All in the Family _Nehemiah 9:34-38_

1. Are there people in my family that I need to make things right with? Name them here.

_____

_____

_____

_____

2. What unfinished business with my family do I need to face as part of my inventory? What about as part of my grieving?

_____

_____

_____

_____

Constructive Sorrow _2 Corinthians 7:8-11_

1. In what ways do I still resist grieving over my loss?

_____

_____

_____

_____

2. Have I been willing to set aside time to grieve? What's stopping me?

_____

_____

_____

_____

3. In my grieving have I been self-condemning? What prevents me from experiencing God's grace?

_____

_____

_____

_____

God's Mercy *Revelation 20:11-15*

1. Taking a moral inventory of yourself here on earth will help to prepare you for the life to come. In what ways do I still resist making an inventory?

_____

_____

_____

_____

2. Write out a prayer of trust and willingness to complete Step Four.

_____

_____

_____

_____

3. Write out another prayer to God that expresses your complete dependence upon him for salvation, and ask him to walk with you through the grieving process.

_____

_____

_____

_____

In Psalm 119:29, the writer pleads with God: "Keep me from lying to myself." Our inventories, when compiled with honesty and diligence, are the beginning of facing the truth about our need to grow in character and maturity in spite of our losses. It is welcoming the new, authentic you.

PROFILE

Rich knew he was on thin ice at his work. For the past six months, since his promotion, he struggled with his new responsibilities. He thought management was working with him to overcome his struggles with the job, but one Friday they terminated him and escorted him out of the building. He kind of expected it might happen, but he had no idea it would be so humiliating and devastating.

Rich had been working in his field for twenty-five years. He knew the industry and was well-known and respected. He had had smooth sailing up until this last promotion. It seemed to him that what he had built over those twenty-five years was totally destroyed this fateful Friday.

As he sat in his car, Rich's next thought was about how he could possibly bear to tell his wife. It wasn't that he feared her response: She had always been very supportive and understanding. He was more concerned with how he was going to admit to her that he was a failure, because that's what he was feeling as he sat there, like a total and complete failure.

Rich was given a decent severance package that included counseling, but it didn't help his feelings of failure. One of the things people fear the most is being seen as a failure, and that's how Rich interpreted the action the company took against him. He was immobilized by his fear. His fear even became panic on several subsequent occasions. When people asked him how he was feeling, his typical response was that he felt like somebody had just socked him in the stomach and he couldn't catch his breath. He withdrew from all social contact with friends. His wife walked on eggshells around him because she didn't know how to help him.

All of his life, Rich had defined himself through his work. If you had asked him who he was, he would describe himself as part of his industry. That's why he took his termination so personally. Four months into what he called his "forced retirement," his wife reminded him of the offer of counseling in the severance package. She even threatened to leave if he didn't make an appointment and go. The counselor talked to him about his need to grieve for what he had lost, and then reminded him that what Rich had truly lost was his identity. Then the counselor explained the process of grieving to him.

Rich was finally able to feel angry over what had happened to him. He also examined his anger at himself for not paying attention to the signs that things were not going well with his job. As he identified his losses—his identity, friends at work, a sense of purpose, his self-confidence—and processed his sadness, he gradually experienced a lifting of his depression.

STEP FIVE

We admitted to God, to ourselves, and to another human being the exact nature of our wrongs.

Doing a fearless moral inventory is not a simple task. It isn't something we can do in a couple minutes. To look deeply into ourselves takes time and courage. Some people never get to Step Five because they simply give up and don't even try Step Four. But we were fearless, and we did our inventories—both a moral inventory and a "new normal you" inventory. Now we must do something equally difficult. We must confess our wrongdoings. Admitting to God is one thing, but telling another person takes it to a whole different level. If we have to admit everything to someone else, we'll be found out. We'd much rather keep our inventories secret.

This step comes directly from James 5:16: "Confess your sins to each other and pray for each other so that you may be healed." Confession has been practiced throughout the history of the church in many different ways. Today, in many of our Christian communities, confessing to our fellow Christians has fallen out of practice in favor of only confessing to God. We feel vulnerable and exposed and embarrassed when we tell other people what we've done wrong. It's crucially important for our salvation that we confess our sins to God. But James makes a very important connection between our confessing our sins to one another and our ability to be healed.

Without confession to God and to one another, we cannot experience full healing. Without healing, our grief and our sins continue to fester. In Jeremiah 6:14 the prophet says, "They offer superficial treatments for my people's mortal wound. They give assurances of peace when there is no peace." Here's how *The Living Bible* paraphrased this verse: "You can't heal a wound by saying it's not there!" There is something important about confessing to another person that plays a key role in our healing.

Step Five uses the word *admitted*, and the Bible uses the word *confess*, but they mean essentially the same thing. When we confess, we admit that we agree with what happened. We align ourselves with the truth, and we align ourselves with God.

To work Step Five, we must reach another level of humility and willingness. To have God in all parts of our hearts and lives, we must be able to admit our exact wrongs honestly and openly. By sharing our story of poor choices, poor relationships, and poor reactions to our life circumstances, we get a clearer picture of ourselves. This confessional step initiates a new direction in our lives as we begin to live in a way that seeks to please the Spirit of God and harvest everlasting life.

Who should this person be to whom we will entrust our moral inventory and our "new normal you" inventory? Who can we trust to be part of our healing process? Jesus is our model for the type of person we should seek. We need someone who is more interested in our spiritual wholeness and our freedom and progress in recovery than in the individual issues we share. Ideally, we can find someone who has been through the Twelve Steps personally and who can listen with compassion and acceptance, not with judgment. When we have completed this step, we may have a mixture of feelings, from relief to gratitude to confusion. We have now inventoried and disclosed our deepest moral and spiritual secrets. We have faced some difficult aspects of ourselves that we have wanted to deny before. We have bravely charted the course for the "new normal you" in our lives. Adhering to this process is an additional surrender in itself.

In terms of our fearless moral inventories, if we confess the exact nature of our wrongs to ourselves, to God, and to another human being, God not only forgives everything we confess, but he also cleanses us of all the wrong things we have done that we may not even realize. This truth is expressed in 1 John 1:9, which says: "If we confess our sins to him, he is faithful and just to forgive us our sins and to cleanse us from all wickedness." What a great promise for those who confess!

QUESTIONS FOR **STEP FIVE**

Overcoming Denial *Genesis 38:1-30*

1. What am I avoiding in Step Four by delaying Step Five?

_____

_____

_____

_____

2. What is the exact nature of my wrongs as listed in my fearless moral inventory?

_____

_____

_____

_____

3. Why am I afraid to have someone hear my confession of my "new normal you" inventory?

_____

_____

_____

_____

4. What interferes with being honest about myself?

_____

_____

_____

_____

Crying Out to God *Psalm 38:9-16*

1. To some people, grieving is like a disease. They are afraid of it. Has anyone withdrawn from me because they believed that? How did that make me feel?

_____

_____

_____

_____

2. Have I felt abandoned in my grief? What do I do with my feelings of abandonment?

_____

_____

_____

_____

_____

3. How do I keep focused on God, who always understands the pain of my grief?

_____

_____

_____

_____

Joyful Confession _Isaiah 43:25–44:5_

1. In what ways does my life feel like a parched field?

_____

_____

_____

_____

2. In what ways have I neglected to feed my spirit?

_____

_____

_____

_____

3. In what ways have I experienced God's longing to replenish my life?

_____

_____

_____

4. Have I set the appointment for completing Step Five by sharing my Step Four inventory? My commitment to myself:

Date   Time   Who

_____

_____

_____

Covenant Love *Hosea 11:8-11*

1. How do I react or respond to the truth that God does not give up on me?

_____

_____

_____

2. What keeps me from being truthful with God?

_____

_____

_____

3. What makes me think I can hide anything from God?

_____

_____

_____

The Plumb Line *Amos 7:7-8*

1. Have my morals and values been in line with God's? Explain.

_____

_____

_____

_____

2. Where have I had difficulty applying my morals and values in my life?

_____

_____

_____

3. What has kept me from staying in line with God's and my own morals and values?

_____

_____

_____

4. Am I ready to surrender to God's moral plumb line? If not, why am I hesitating?

_____

_____

_____

*There is a lifting of a great
weight when we confess.*

PROFILE

In his memoir *The Sacred Journey*, Frederick Buechner describes the day his father committed suicide. He writes that he and his brother woke early and "there was no going back to sleep again because immediately all the excitement of the day that was about to be burst in upon us like the sun itself, and we could not conceivably have closed our eyes on it."* He was talking about his parents taking him and his brother to a football game. Their grandmother was visiting as well. So to pass the morning, the two brothers sat on the floor of the bedroom playing a game.

A little while later the bedroom door opened slightly, and somebody silently looked in on them—their father. Later on, they could not remember any other details, even when they finally got around to sharing their memories of it many years later. After their father looked in on them, he apparently went down to the garage and committed suicide. They found him lying on the garage floor and the car engine running. They threw open the garage doors and called the doctor, but it was too late. A couple days later they found a goodbye note written on the last page of the book he had been reading.

There was no time to grieve because his mother gathered the two boys soon after and moved to Bermuda in an effort to leave

---

* Frederick Buechner, *The Sacred Journey* (San Francisco, CA: Harper & Row, 1982), 37.

it all behind them. About a year later, Buechner came upon his brother crying all by himself in his room. He writes,

> I was stopped dead in my tracks. Why was he crying? When I prodded him into telling me that he was crying about something that he would not name but said only had happened a long time ago, I finally knew what he meant, and I can recapture still my astonishment that, for him, a wound was still open that for me, or so I thought, has long since closed.*

It was years before Buechner dealt emotionally with his father's suicide. He was a writer, but for years he didn't write about it or talk about it. When he did finally write about it, his mother was livid. It was a family secret that was meant to remain concealed, but he had violated that rule. In several of his subsequent books, it was like he couldn't help but refer to that fateful day.

Carl's story is different. When his favorite cousin committed suicide, it was no secret. It was part of the public dialogue from the first moment he heard about it. And when Carl called his best friend for support, he could barely get the words out between his sobs. His emotions were all mixed up. He was angry at his cousin, alternating between raging at his friend for the stupidity of what his cousin had done and sobbing in sadness.

When Carl sat down with his friend, he still couldn't grasp that it had happened. He said his cousin had just started a new job and loved it. He had booked a vacation with several of his friends. To Carl, his cousin seemed to have all kinds of things to live for. Carl was filled with why questions: "Why now?" "Will he go to heaven?" "Why didn't he talk to me about his feelings?" "Everything seemed to be starting to go his way, so why?" "I thought we were closer than that." All this questioning only made Carl more frustrated, angry, and helpless. Suicide never makes any sense. And that makes it even harder to grieve.

---

* Ibid., 42.

Suicide catches us unaware because it often happens when the person is starting to feel better. What's deceiving is that when they start to feel better, they can make especially bad decisions. To the survivors, it is always an irrational act, and there are no answers to the *why* questions. Carl, in his grieving, had to come to a point of acceptance without understanding to be able to complete the process of grieving.

STEP SIX
We were entirely ready to have God remove these defects of character.

Step Six is a pause in the process of the Twelve Steps. There is nothing that we do, no action we take in this step. It's for "getting ready." Before we can experience behavioral changes in our lives, we first need to experience a change in our hearts. In Hebrew, the language of the Old Testament, the word for *heart* refers to the center of our being. That's why we can say our grief comes from the heart—the center of who we are.

Our willingness to change is the point of this step, just as it was the point of Jesus' encounter with the man at the pool of Bethesda, as described in John 5. The man Jesus talks to has been at that pool for thirty-eight years. It was his home. It was where his friends were. It was the center of his life. So it was a serious question when Jesus asked him, "Would you like to get well?" (John 5:6). If he didn't have to sit at the pool every day, what was he going to do with all of his time? Jesus was asking if the man was willing to have his whole life changed.

The man never directly answered Jesus' question. Instead, he offered a valid excuse. He said he has no one to get him to the water in time to be healed, so he couldn't be healed. For Jesus, the man's response suggested a willingness to change. The man was truly powerless but apparently willing, and so Jesus took what the man couldn't do and did it for him.

This step simply questions our willingness. There's nothing else we need to do for this step. This step is asking: "Are you entirely ready?" The previous two steps examine what needs to be changed in our lives. Here we have a step that merely asks if we're ready.

Why do we need this step? Because the focus is different. It's not asking if we are going to change, as if we were going to do it ourselves. We know that doesn't work because we've tried it in the past. Step Six is asking us if we're ready to do it the right way this time—to let God do the changing.

Why would we not be ready? Some of our character defects have been useful to us, and sometimes those defects have been necessary for survival. It can be very difficult to let them go when they are so automatic and so deeply ingrained in us. This process of becoming "entirely ready" can bring additional grief. It's grieving our loss of a loved one, as well as letting go of old friends and our old ways of life. This is especially true of the "new normal you" inventory. Sometimes when we grieve, we don't want to move forward because that means we have to let go of the past and our loved one. But grief is supposed to be a process, not a persistent way of life.

Our inventory was only the first half of the process by which we practice character building. Now we must begin to allow God's Spirit to work deeply in our hearts, rooting out our defects of character by making changes in our behaviors and attitudes that will bring wholesomeness and serenity.

We also need to see that this isn't an all-or-nothing step, even though it may feel that way. Remember it's a step about *willingness*. Are you willing to change? It's like what the apostle Paul said about his personal journey: "I don't mean to say that I have already achieved these things or that I have already reached perfection. But I press on to possess that perfection for which Christ Jesus first possessed me" (Philippians 3:12). Paul's reference to perfection is not what we think of when we think of perfection. Paul is simply talking about his progress toward the goal of excellence—being everything God wants him to be.

That's the way it is with Step Six. It's like we're on the edge of a new phase in our life. Up to this point, we were wrestling with the decision to surrender our character defects and our previous way of life. Our attitude is the main thing. This is the step where we are asked to take ownership of our character defects and our losses. It's wishful thinking that God will just take them away. When we are willing to give them up, we become a part of a special process. It's a simple formula: Sin is the problem, Jesus is the cure, and the result is a miracle.

The key to this step is for us to have a "broken and repentant heart" (Psalm 51:17). When King David finally faced himself, he realized that nothing had given him the key to success in God's eyes—not his pride, his position in life, or his previous successes. It was only through his brokenness that he was able to experience success in living according to God's standard. God loves us with a faithful love, but his love for us is more fully experienced when we come to him in an attitude of humility and brokenness. The early developers of the Twelve Steps called this step the Step of Repentance. They believed that repentance meant turning around and going in a different direction. That's what Step Six calls for: a change of direction!

QUESTIONS FOR **STEP SIX**

Time to Grieve *Genesis 23:1-4; 35:19-21*

1. What is standing in my way of being able to grieve? Make a list of losses.

_____

_____

_____

_____

2. What defects of character are standing in my way of
   grieving?

_____

_____

_____

Healing Our Brokenness *Psalm 51:16-19*

1. How have the last five steps prepared me to be "entirely
   ready" for God to work in my heart?

_____

_____

_____

2. In this psalm, David had to grow up a little. He had to accept
   that he was flawed in God's eyes and that he could never
   bring a sacrifice good or perfect enough to atone for those
   flaws. Am I still trying to bring God evidence of how good I
   am, or am I coming to a place of acceptance, as David did?
   How does acceptance help me to stay in the grieving process? Explain.

_____

_____

_____

3. Jesus says: "God blesses those who mourn, for they will
   be comforted" (Matthew 5:4). In what ways has God comforted me?

_____

_____

_____

God's Abundant Pardon *Isaiah 55:1-9*

1. What ways have I tried to fill the hunger of my soul and the thirst of my spirit with activity instead of trusting in following God's will?

_____

_____

_____

2. Do I believe in my heart, not just in my head, that the life God has for me in the future will be even more satisfying than the one I've lived up to this point? Is my heart willing to believe this?

_____

_____

_____

Going Deeper *Jonah 4:4-8*

1. What deeper problems did my loss uncover? Fear? Pride? Egocentrism? Anger? Hatred? The arrogance of believing that life should go the way I want?

_____

_____

_____

2. What difficulties have I suffered that have revealed deeper hurts?

_____

_____

_____

3. Am I willing to have these defects removed by God? Why or why not?

_____

_____

_____

_____

Discovering Hope _John 5:1-15_

When we are ready, God does his part. Our part is to get rid of excuses, stubborn resistance, holding on to the familiar, and our fear of change. When we clear out these blocks and become entirely ready, it becomes clear that God must do the rest, because only he can accomplish the miracle of setting our feet on the path of an authentic life again.

1. What have been my excuses for not moving forward in my recovery?

_____

_____

_____

_____

_____

2. Have I been stubbornly resistant because I've been afraid of change? Why?

_____

_____

_____

_____

_____

Attitudes and Actions *Philippians 3:12-14*

This is the attitude of Step Six: "Work hard to show the results of your salvation, obeying God with deep reverence and fear. For God is working in you, giving you the desire and the power to do what pleases him" (Philippians 2:12-13).

1. Do I have a vision for the purposes for which God saved me spiritually? Describe it.

_____

_____

_____

_____

2. Am I now willing to accept that I will continue taking this step in order to grow, letting go of the old way of life to make room for the "new normal you"? Why or why not?

_____

_____

_____

_____

> *First Peter 4:1 tells us to arm ourselves with*
> *the attitude of Christ, who was prepared and*
> *willing to suffer. It's time to get ready.*

S T E P **7**

PROFILE

Roger hadn't spoken to his father in over eight years. They had a big blowup eight years ago, and neither one would give an inch, so they just stayed away from each other. His father was now in his mid-eighties, and Roger felt that he should make amends before his father died. Lately, Roger was feeling an increasing sense of urgency to meet with his dad. He made a vow to himself that when he got back from his current business trip, he would set up a meeting with his father.

Soon after he arrived in Europe, he got a text from his brother that his dad had had what he called a "heart episode." It wasn't a heart attack, but it was serious, especially at his dad's age. Roger canceled the rest of his business trip and booked a flight back home. As he was driving home from the airport, he got a text from his brother saying that his father had just died.

If Roger could have kicked himself, he would have. He was extremely frustrated, berating himself for putting off the meeting with his father. Now it was too late. It all felt hopeless to him. He would never have the chance to make things right with his father. He was like many others he knew who rushed to their dying parent's bedside only to arrive too late.

Roger realized that he was stuck in his remorse, so he called his counselor and made an appointment. He knew he was going to need help with this. He tried to tell the counselor about his anger with himself over delaying the meeting. He went into detail about what had happened eight years ago, and the counselor listened closely.

Finally the counselor spoke up and told Roger, "You know it's not your actual father that you're dealing with; it's the father that lives in your head." The counselor then set out to explain to Roger what he meant. He talked about how the battle with his father was always going on in his head. It had been going on for eight years. That's where Roger rehearsed the argument he had with his father over and over, where he could even hear his father's voice argue against him. The counselor pointed out that this was the father he needed to make amends with.

The counselor suggested that Roger write his father a letter where he explained all the things that he wanted to say to his father in person. Then Roger was to read the letter to an empty chair, with his wife sitting there with him. He might even put a picture of his father on the empty chair. Or they could go to his father's graveside and read the letter there. It could be a real emotional experience that would bring closure to the issue for Roger because he would really be reading the letter to the father that lived in his head.

Roger spent several weeks writing the letter. He decided to go to the graveside to read it to him. His wife joined him for emotional support; it surprised him how emotional he got as he wrote the letter. When Roger finished reading the letter, he and his wife talked about it a bit, and then he burned the letter, leaving the ashes on his father's grave.

STEP SEVEN

We humbly asked God to remove our shortcomings.

Step Seven proves the wisdom of working the steps in order from the beginning. Some people just want to jump in anywhere that strikes their fancy. When they do that, their recovery is really neither a process nor a path. This is especially true for Step Seven, which is the culmination of Steps Four through Six. Our pathway begins with the readiness and willingness to have our defects removed by God. Before we can be ready and willing, we have to do the Step Four inventories, then we can admit the truth to ourselves, to God, and to another person. These steps bring clarity to our lives and become the foundation for the rest of our journey. Now our willingness becomes a request that God remove our defects.

That makes this step one of the easiest to do and in other ways, the hardest. We are asking God to do the work. This will mark a turning point in our recovery. Now we begin to allow God's Spirit to flow into our lives and replace character defects with character strengths. We get out of our own way and literally give control to God.

It's important to understand that God isn't going to fix us instantly. The truth is that God has a very different plan. His plan will involve other people, tough experiences, and hard decisions. He knows what it takes to change people with potential into people who grow, relate, and make changes the way God wants.

The problem with instant change is that it never brings instant character nor does it help us mature. That's what recovery is all about. It's about our maturing and developing character. It does take time, and God knows that. The other point that's important to make at this juncture is that God doesn't deal with everybody the same way. And if we want to determine how God is going to work in us, we have forgotten the early lesson that we are powerless without him and that we turned our wills and our lives over to him.

God's plan is often the work of *opposites*. He challenges us to rely upon him and to ask the Holy Spirit for the power to do the opposite of what we are accustomed to doing. We may argue with our impulses, but then we humbly ask God to give us the strength to move in the opposite direction. We may not have thought well of groups in which people share the intimate details of their lives. Now we have to stop ridiculing those people and do the opposite—become part of them. Over and over doing the opposite of what we would do when left to our own devices becomes our goal.

This step begins with the word *humbly*. Our first taste of humility was when we admitted our powerlessness. Now we see that this is just the beginning of a lifelong process in which God brings us closer to his image and purpose. In terms of our grieving, humility is also a factor. A big part of our grieving is realizing how powerless we are. It takes humility in grieving to allow God to be God, not to simply be our adversary. Remember, God's questioning of Job was to increase Job's humility and to let God be God. And in our grieving, we are learning new things about ourselves as well. Know this: God is always up to something good. For as Paul says, "we can be so sure that every detail in our lives of love for God is worked into something good" (Romans 8:28, MSG).

QUESTIONS FOR **STEP SEVEN**

Clearing the Mess *Isaiah 57:12-19*

1. Have I developed enough humility from my experiences to see that I need to let God work in my heart? Is there any doubt that self-reliance has kept God out?

_____

_____

_____

_____

_____

2. Describe the difference between humiliation and humility.

_____

_____

_____

_____

Giving Up Control *Jeremiah 18:1-6*

1. Have I ever demanded that God change circumstances for my benefit? When?

_____

_____

_____

_____

2. Have I ever been impatient about God's timing?

_____

_____

_____

_____

3. What keeps me from letting go so that God can change my life?

_____

_____

_____

_____

4. In my grieving, have I become impatient with God?

_____

_____

_____

_____

Pride Born of Hurt _Luke 11:5-13_

1. Is it hard for me to ask anyone, even God, for help? If so, why?

_____

_____

_____

_____

2. How has that affected my grieving process?

_____

_____

_____

_____

3. What experiences in my family brought about my self-sufficiency?

_____

_____

_____

_____

4. Do I trust God to meet my needs and to walk with me through my grief? Why or why not?

_____

_____

_____

_____

A Humble Heart _Luke 18:10-14_

1. Have I ever compared my faults, problems, losses, and sins to blatant sins of others in order to avoid deeper work on my own character defects? What does this do for me?

_____

_____

_____

_____

2. While grieving, have I struggled at all with self-hatred or self-harm? What do I need to do in order to be open with a trusted adviser or counselor about this?

_____

_____

_____

_____

3. Am I humble enough to let others know that I'm grieving?

_____

_____

_____

_____

An Open Book *Philippians 2:5-9*

1. How important is my image to me?

_____

_____

_____

2. Can I release to God my self-centered fears of being known and of losing my image? Write a prayer to God expressing the desire to do so.

_____

_____

_____

Unending Love *1 John 5:1-15*

1. What blocks me from asking God to do the work of character building and maturity in my heart and life? Describe each block.

_____

_____

_____

_____

2. How confident am I in believing that God is willing to remove my shortcomings? Describe those feelings.

_____

_____

_____

_____

Shortcomings is a very polite way of describing sin, weakness, defects in character, addiction, compulsions, dependency, or a thousand other conditions and symptoms that indicate we are falling short of the glory of God and the lives he has called us to live. Asking God to remove our shortcomings is always a joint venture between us and him. Since we have spent much of our lives proving we can't fix ourselves, it is time to finally ask God to do what we will never have the power or insight to do ourselves.

A Prayer for Step Seven

Dear God,
Search my heart and reveal to me any arrogance or pride that is separating me from you, the people around me, and the person you have called me to be. My shortcomings are numerous, and my attempts to fix them always end in failure. Please remove these shortcomings from me. Do for me what I cannot do for myself. Give me the courage to do whatever it takes to become victorious over these problems. Thank you for the work you are doing in me and for the opportunity to transform my life. Amen.

PROFILE

Tom and Deanna had been married for twenty-one years. They had two daughters in high school. They always thought they were a typical family—no major problems, financially secure, kids who behaved well. But recently Tom had been acting a little strange. He started combing his hair differently, then he got a different kind of haircut. He started exercising and losing weight. But to Deanna these were not the most troubling symptoms. She was concerned because he was becoming more secretive about his life.

Deanna became suspicious—not overly so, but a little bit more every day. Gradually, her suspicion grew. When Tom lied to her about where he had been, she finally admitted to herself that something was going on, and she didn't like it. As she began to quietly double-check her husband's plans more and more, she kept finding more inconsistencies in Tom's behavior. Finally she started listening to her intuition and took the risk of confronting Tom. This led to a shouting match, and Tom grabbed some clothes and left their home.

Tom stayed away for three days, and when Deanna was at work, he went back home, packed up all of his things, and moved in with his girlfriend. So it was obvious now that he had been having an affair.

Deanna was crushed. She never even entertained the thought that this might happen in her marriage: Tom just wasn't that kind of guy. But apparently he was. It felt like Deanna's life was being ripped to pieces.

Deanna was paralyzed with an incredible sadness. She still went to work, but at home it was all she could do to take care of her daughters. She cried herself to sleep every night. As the weeks turned into months with no changes in Tom's behavior, a close friend told Deanna she needed to grieve her marriage and her old life. It looked like the marriage was over, and it was time to look at what had been lost. On the weekends her friend would come to visit, and together they started to enumerate the losses. It looked like Deanna had lost her marriage, her dream of an intact family, her role as a wife, the security of a financially stable future, and Tom himself—the most significant loss.

As Deanna and her friend met, they talked and prayed together. Deanna finally admitted that she felt guilty about feeling angry. Her friend wisely responded to that by asking Deanna if a lot of her anger was directed inwardly at herself? Deanna agreed that she was stuck in the grieving process because she was obsessed with the thought that she should have done something to stop this. She should have known earlier, she should've been paying more attention to their marriage, and she should have been a better wife. Fortunately, Deanna had someone to grieve with her, and she was navigating the journey of grieving successfully. She realized now that not all losses are caused by death.

STEP EIGHT

We made a list of all persons we had harmed and became willing to make amends to them all.

Our first reaction when reading this step might be: "It's in the past; it's over and done with. Nothing can be done about it now." But it's often not over. If we don't deal with our past issues, then they can be easily reawakened by events in our present. Step Eight is the only way to deal with our issues in the present and leave them in the past. When that is done, we become open to looking outside of ourselves and moving into healed and restored relationships. It all begins with a list.

Lists are valuable parts of the Twelve Steps. In Step Four, we listed all the shortcomings and defects we knew about ourselves. Now we need to make a list of people who have been affected by those shortcomings and defects. This will be a list of people we know we have harmed. More than anything, it is a list of relationships that may be healed and restored when we honestly seek to make amends for what we have said and done to hurt others.

Some people's names will be on our list because what we have done against them is so large that it cannot be ignored. There will also be people on the list who might not be as obvious—those who have felt rejected or abandoned by us. No matter how big or how small the offense, we must record the names of those who most likely do not think fondly of us or of their time with us.

This step is a tough way of carrying out Luke 6:31: "Do to others as you would like them to do to you." Wouldn't we all love to get a call or letter from someone who hurt us and hear him or her express regret and remorse? Wouldn't we love to know that, in the end, this person was not gloating over what was done to us, but instead wanted to make it right? Such restitution has rarely happened in our lives because so few people can humble themselves enough to admit they were wrong, let alone be willing to make amends to those who paid the price for their actions.

Once our lists are complete, we must once again exercise our will. Each entry may come with a host of excuses for why we should not make amends. But take note that this step includes a very significant word: *all.* Our willingness to make amends must encompass every entry on our lists, even if later we might discover some valid reasons for why it wouldn't be wise or helpful to make amends to everyone we have harmed.

This step is only for making the list and for becoming willing to make amends. Once we have made the list as complete as possible at this time, that's all we have to do for this step. The decision about whether to make amends with someone is part of the next step.

Willingness is a huge aspect of all facets of recovery. We cannot work on any of the steps without being willing. And we cannot work any of the steps well unless and until we have come to the place where we are willing to do whatever it takes to recover or work though our grief.

A big part of our grieving has to do with a willingness to move forward in the process with someone. This can be a problem for couples, for often husbands and wives grieve differently. Because of this, our grieving partner will often be a good friend or a sensitive relative.

One thing to watch out for at this step of the grieving process is rationalization. We can rationalize a lot of people off our lists by focusing on what they did to us or changing their horrible act into a merely crummy act. Focus on your own behavior in relationship to that person. Another caution has to do with defensiveness. It is easy to obsess about the fact that they should be contacting us and to decide that the other person should be the one to make the first move. We have to get beyond our naturally defensive thoughts and focus on our own responsibility.

One more thing: Often when we make a list of people we have hurt, we leave off the person who has experienced more pain than anyone else—*ourselves*. You must acknowledge that you have hurt yourself, and you must put your name at the top of the list of people you have harmed. Willingness to forgive ourselves and make amends to ourselves makes it easier to do the same for others.

QUESTIONS FOR **STEP EIGHT**

Making Restitution *Exodus 22:10-15*

1. How have I failed to respect the property of others?

_____

_____

_____

_____

2. How have I avoided responsibility?

_____

_____

_____

_____

3. What excuses have I used for not looking at my own behaviors?

_____

_____

_____

_____

Unintentional Sins *Leviticus 4:1-28*

1. In what ways have I unintentionally harmed others with my words, moods, self-pity, depression, anger, or fears?

_____

_____

_____

_____

2. In what ways have I acted thoughtlessly, without regard for others' needs or feelings?

_____

_____

_____

_____

Scapegoats _Leviticus 16:20-22_

1. Have I been putting off making a list because I am afraid of some responses? Who am I afraid of? Why?

_____

_____

_____

_____

2. Is there someone I'm having trouble forgiving who blocks my willingness to work through this step? Who?

_____

_____

_____

_____

Coming Out of Isolation _Ecclesiastes 4:9-12_

1. How have I allowed isolation to block or slow down my grieving process?

_____

_____

_____

_____

2. What is the role of shame and guilt in my isolation?

_____

_____

_____

_____

3. Am I willing to forgive myself for the hurt I've caused others? How about forgiving myself for the hurt I have caused myself? Write a prayer of willingness to forgive.

_____

_____

_____

_____

Forgiving Others, Forgiving Yourself _Matthew 18:23-35_

1. Are there people on my list who I am having trouble forgiving for their part in our relationship? Who and why?

_____

_____

_____

_____

2. What stops me from letting others off the hook? Fear? Resentment? Care-taking?

_____

_____

_____

_____

3. What blocks me from forgiving others for the wrongs they have done to me?

   a. Fear of what others would think of me?

   _____

   _____

   b. Fear of letting others see my hurts?

   _____

   _____

   c. Fear of conflict? Protecting others' feelings to avoid conflict?

   _____

   _____

Grace-Filled Living *2 Corinthians 2:5-8*

1. Is there anyone, either on my list or not, whose behaviors I do not approve of? Who? Why?

   _____

   _____

   _____

   _____

2. Am I willing to let go of judgment and disapproval to open myself to the grieving process and to working this step?

   _____

   _____

   _____

   _____

3. Have I been so afraid of rejection that I have delayed my grieving process? What about my willingness to make amends?

_____

_____

_____

_____

Remember: It's about willingness!

PROFILE

They seemed like a quiet family. In fact, Jack and Sadie seemed like the perfect couple. They had two children, one in elementary school and the other in middle school, and what seemed like a normal and happy family.

But one night was obviously different. Jack not only lost his temper, but he also lost his wife. Jack and Sadie had gotten into a big argument; then Jack took out his gun and pointed it at Sadie—meaning only to threaten her—but the gun suddenly went off, and Sadie lay on the floor dying. She was pronounced dead on the way to the hospital, and Jack was quickly arrested. As the media interviewed neighbors the next day, they asked if Jack had ever shown signs of an out-of-control temper. To a person, everyone agreed that they were totally surprised by the event. No one had ever witnessed Jack losing his temper.

To say that Sadie's parents, Travis and Maria, were shocked would be an understatement. They surmised from guarded conversations with their daughter that Jack had a problem with his anger, but nothing like this! Only when they had to identify their daughter's body did reality set in.

When Jack was arraigned and charged, Travis and Maria were in the audience. During his trial, they were in the audience every day. Not only were they in the audience, but they talked with Jack at breaks. Somehow Travis and Maria had pulled themselves together in order to be present and, in some strange way, to show their support for Jack.

During this time, Travis and Maria determined that they would turn their misery into a ministry. They forgave Jack and began speaking publicly about the meaning of forgiveness. They developed quite a ministry out of sharing their story of how they had forgiven their son-in-law who murdered their daughter.

I (Dave) invited them to the Caring Friends group (a grief support group run by a local church for parents whose children have died), but they declined by saying they didn't need to come. Several years later, I was on a local television program talking about the process of forgiveness. Maria was also there telling about how she and her husband had forgiven their son-in-law after he had killed their daughter. During a break, I had the chance to talk with Maria. I told her how I had always been bothered by how quickly they forgave their son-in-law. It was like they never processed their grief.

Maria said, "No, we processed our grief just as you described." Then she said something I've never forgotten: "We just made the decision at the beginning that we were going to forgive Jack. It took us a long time to finish the forgiving process. In fact, it would be legitimate to say we've never really stopped grieving."

Based on that conversation, I have divided the forgiveness stage of grieving into three parts: First we make the decision to forgive. Then we process the emotions of anger as protest and the sadness of resignation through our grieving. And finally, we forgive completely.

STEP NINE

We made direct amends to such people wherever possible, except when to do so would injure them or others.

You may notice that in Step Nine, we put into practice the principles of the previous eight steps: powerlessness, restoration to sanity, willingness, and seeking help. Now we add the important principle of making amends.

The word *amend* means "to put right or to change." That means we are not talking about a simple apology; we are talking about a serious change of attitude on our part where we also admit to causing pain and loss in another person. Unless we confess our wrongs to at least one other person, we will find our healing incomplete. If we can talk, write, phone, text, or email the person we have harmed, we need to do so. If the person is dead or cannot be located or contacted, we need to at least confess to another person to get the secret out. Finally, if we cannot make amends directly to the person we harmed, perhaps we can make amends in another way.

In Genesis 32–33, we see this step in action. When Jacob had to flee his home because he feared that his brother would kill him, he stayed away for many years. Then God directed him to go home. On his way home, Jacob reached out to his brother in peace because he hoped that Esau would be friendly (Genesis 32:5). Clearly Jacob was still afraid that Esau would kill him. When Esau responds to Jacob's message by meeting him with an army of 400 men, Jacob was afraid (Genesis 32:6-7). Jacob had no idea whether his brother intended to kill him or had put Jacob's offenses out of his mind.

So Jacob determined to make amends to his brother, Esau, by sending ahead of his group herds of various livestock as a gift (Genesis 32:13-16). To Jacob's surprise, after he bowed to the ground seven times before Esau, Esau ran to meet him and embraced him (Genesis 33:3-4). Esau asked Jacob, "'What were all the flocks and herds I met as I came?' . . . Jacob replied, 'They are a gift, my lord, to ensure your friendship'" (Genesis 33:8). Even though Esau wasn't going to kill him anymore, Jacob still made his amends to Esau.

We don't know what Esau's intentions were when he brought 400 men with him to meet his brother, Jacob. And Esau had no idea what Jacob's intentions were when he came home. But Jacob knew he had harmed his brother—which is why he had to leave home in the first place—and he was ready to make amends regardless of his brother's intentions.

This step also includes a qualifier—*except when to do so would injure them or others*—that can be wrongly used as an excuse not to make amends, rather than as a protection for those who have been hurt. It can allow us to walk away from life-changing opportunities, for ourselves and for others.

If the person we have sinned against is too weak or sensitive or wounded, and he or she may be hurt further by our confession, then perhaps this is not the right time to confess. Nevertheless, we can begin to work toward making amends when it is the right time. And when the time comes, we do not necessarily have to tell the truth one-on-one or alone. We may need the help of a counselor to make the process go as well as possible. We may also need the counselor's help in teaching us the language of forgiveness. The resolution may not be quick, but we should strive to make it happen at the most effective time possible.

This is a very tough step, but in some ways it makes more sense than any other step. At least the purpose is easier to understand. Quite simply, it is not enough in every case for us to apologize for what we have taken from others without offering to make restitution. It might be enough if they accept the amends but do not want further contact. It might be enough just to say we're sorry if there is no tangible way to make it right. But more often than not, there is a way to make amends that includes complete restoration, especially if two people can work through their differences and resolve the damage and the pain to make things right.

In Matthew 5:23-24, Jesus clearly shows how important this step is to God: "So if you are presenting a sacrifice at the altar in the Temple and you suddenly remember that someone has something against you, leave your sacrifice there at the altar. Go and be reconciled to that person. Then come and offer your sacrifice to God." Here is the God of the universe, who deserves and demands our worship, telling us how important having a clean slate in our relationships is for us to worship rightly.

The amends process and Steps Eight and Nine bring out the "unfinished business" in our lives. We may discover past traumas that must be faced and dealt with if we are to maintain our recovery. It is important not to do this alone but to talk with your counselor or another trusted adviser about what these steps bring to the surface. We may not have caused these traumas to occur, but we may have to make amends to ourselves for allowing past trauma to define us or curtail our lives.

Restoration of relationship with ourselves is an important outcome of Step Nine. There is no more need to run when we have come face-to-face with those we have harmed and have sought to make things right. There is no longer any need to run because the slate is clean. We no longer need to speculate about forgiveness: We have forgiven, and we have received forgiveness.

QUESTIONS FOR **STEP NINE**

A Feared Encounter *Genesis 33:1-11*

1. Who are the people on my Step Eight list who strike the most intense fear in my heart when I think about making amends face-to-face?

_____

_____

_____

_____

2. Do I have support people who will remind me again of my willingness to take such a challenging step?

_____

_____

_____

_____

Keeping Promises *2 Samuel 9:1-9*

1. How has my grieving made me aware of people with whom I need to make amends?

_____

_____

_____

_____

2. Is there anyone to whom I owe amends due to forgetting to fulfill a promise?

_____

_____

_____

_____

Hope for Those Making Amends *Ezekiel 33:10-16*

1. What type of amends listed in Step Eight do I resist? Why?

_____

_____

_____

_____

2. What are the fears that are keeping me from the life-giving process of Step Nine?

_____

_____

_____

_____

Peacemaking _Matthew 5:23-26_

1. Am I a peacekeeper or peacemaker?

_____

_____

_____

_____

2. What is my usual response or reaction to brokenness?

_____

_____

_____

_____

3. Does my amends list include people that have something against me? Does that make it hard for me to have the courage to deal with them?

_____

_____

_____

_____

The Blessing of Giving *Luke 19:1-10*

1. List the financial amends that you owe. Name the people and amounts:

_____

_____

_____

_____

2. Am I willing to go to any lengths to offer amends?

_____

_____

_____

_____

Unfinished Business *Philemon 1:13-16*

1. Have any relationships or past wrongs come to light in the process of grieving where I still need to make amends?

_____

_____

_____

_____

2. Do I have any unfinished business left on my list?

_____

_____

_____

_____

3. Am I waiting for the certainty of forgiveness before I make amends? Why am I afraid of a lack of certainty?

_____

_____

_____

_____

The Servant's Heart _1 Peter 2:18-25_

1. Am I being reluctant to make amends while I am grieving?

_____

_____

_____

_____

2. Do I fear that painful consequences will cause me more suffering? If so, what is the worst that could happen?

_____

_____

_____

_____

3. Which of the Twelve Steps do I need to focus on before making these fearsome amends?

_____

_____

_____

_____

4. Do I trust God's will for me if I follow the challenge of Step Nine?

_____

_____

_____

_____

There is a price to be paid for freedom,
and it is called restitution.

PROFILE

There is a support group at a church near where I (Dave) live called Caring Friends. It exists for anyone, but the primary focus is on parents who have lost children. The church started the group in order to provide needed support for parents struggling with the death of a child. For example, John and Barbara lost their teenage son, Troy. He was a star athlete at his high school and had all kinds of potential for excelling in his sports in college. Troy was a typical athlete in that he loved to work out. "Never to excess, just staying in shape," he used to say.

One day at football practice, he collapsed on the field. By the time the paramedics arrived, even though one of the coaches had performed CPR on him, Troy was dead. His death was attributed to having what's sometimes called an "athlete's heart." He was in great shape physically, but there was a hidden weakness in his heart that struck unexpectedly. Troy was seventeen when he died. John and Barbara felt like the Caring Friends group was the only place they could talk about the loss of their son. They said that after the funeral, friends seemed to stop talking about Troy. "It was almost as if talking about Troy's death was contagious, and something might happen to one of their children," Barbara said.

In conversations with other parents in their group, they decided to create a memorial center for Troy in their home. They created a space in their dining room where they had pictures of Troy with the family, pictures of him playing sports, his trophies and other awards, and several other personal things that reminded them of Troy. They did not want him to be forgotten, especially by the family.

Grieving for the loss of a child is unlike any other form of grieving. It seems to never end. It's so out of order. Parents are supposed to die first. John and Barbara will do better for a while, but then something reminds them of the emptiness of life without their Troy, and suddenly they grieve again almost as deeply as when they first heard about Troy's death. Their grieving is an ongoing process.

Tony and Mary lost their son when he was thirty-five. He was a corporate jet pilot. At the end of one flight, as he approached the local airport, he was following behind a Boeing 757 airplane, which creates quite a lot of turbulence behind it. He lost control, and the plane crashed, killing all who were on board. Tony and Mary thought they were going to be okay after several months. After all, they had him for thirty-five years. But they found their grief was like no other.

Bill and Martha hardly had a chance to get to know their daughter. She died of cancer at the age of four, following a two-year battle with the aggressive disease. Because of the young age of their daughter, they don't have many memories except treatment. But they understood the anguish of both Tony and Mary and John and Barbara. Their stories are all different, the age of the child lost is different, but the pain and anguish are the same. And their stories were reaffirmed by everyone else in the group.

STEP TEN

We continued to take personal inventory, and when we were wrong, promptly admitted it.

Step Ten is the first of three review steps. Steps One through Nine are the heart of the recovery program and process. First we dealt with our relationship with Jesus as our Higher Power and the reality that we are powerless without him. Then we worked through Steps Four through Seven in order to know ourselves better, more deeply, and more honestly, and we asked God to remove our character defects. Then in Steps Eight and Nine, we sought to make things right with everyone else in our lives. What more is there? Only to continue the process! Recovering from our grief is a continual process that can last a lifetime. And Step Ten continues the path and the process of knowing ourselves that was started in Steps Four through Seven.

Working through Step Ten requires that we know where to work and where to look for the areas that need our attention. When we see patterns and frequent repetition in our behaviors, we realize that these are symptoms indicating that our recovery is lacking in some way. If we neglect or refuse to monitor our behavior, review artifacts, and make amends when necessary, we may have stopped our problem behaviors, but we have short-circuited our recovery and are not really living the life we could be.

The first principle of an ongoing and effective recovery is *honesty*. To be honest, we must embrace *transparency* and *authenticity*. We must give up the need to create illusions designed to convince people that things are not as they appear. We must refuse to allow our lives to be governed by fraud, double-dealing, or trickery. We work to root out any kind of deceit because we know that godly character has no need for deception. Proverbs 23:23 challenges us to "get the truth and never sell it." That includes the truth about ourselves.

Another area to review is the level of *striving* in all aspects of our lives. Are we striving to earn favor with God? Are we demanding of others because we are striving to achieve something beyond our capacity? Are we so perfectionistic that we exhaust ourselves trying to get everything just right so we will look good and feel in total control? In our striving, we become pressured by what we think we ought to do and by what others tell us we ought to do. Life becomes a tyranny of "the shoulds" as we continually *strive* to do more, be more, or meet some incomprehensible demand. It never subsides. Psalm 46:10 clearly tells us what God thinks about striving: "Cease *striving* and know that I am God" (NASB). When we stop trying to do things on our own, we renew our commitment to surrender.

This step is also written to remind us that we are human beings, that we will frequently be wrong. This step does not say *if* but *when* we are wrong. This also levels our pride and helps to keep us emotionally right.

This step also uses the word *promptly*, for the human tendency is to delay, delay, and then delay some more. We delay the recognition of our wrongs and faults. We also delay letting anyone know our wrongs. If we promptly admit and correct ourselves, we prevent these diseased thoughts from taking hold in our minds and hearts, and we can stay close to God. That's why James told us to confess our sins to one another (see James 5:16).

We must never give up or think we have arrived in our following of Step Ten. If we make it a habit to do a quick inventory daily and promptly admit when we are wrong, it isn't that hard to stay the course. When we suffer or even when we are grieving, it's too easy to start grumbling and complaining and asking "why me?" We need to reject and reform that old habit. The admission of our faults and the willingness to correct our wrongs brings eternal rewards.

When we understand and deal with our own faults, then we become free to offer grace to others who need a break. Kindness, tenderness, and forgiveness are the essentials for a life of serenity. When our ongoing inventories reveal that we've strayed from the path of kindness, tenderness, and forgiveness, it's time to reassess our progress and do what we need to do to get back on track.

The apostle Paul warned: "If you think you are standing strong, be careful not to fall" (1 Corinthians 10:12). The best way to avoid falling is to take a regular inventory. And when we are wrong, humbly admit it and make it right.

QUESTIONS FOR **STEP TEN**

Setting Personal Boundaries *Genesis 31:45-55*

1. In order to restore trust in some of my relationships, what particular weaknesses do I need to set boundaries around?

_____

_____

_____

_____

2. Is there a trusted person to whom I can clearly define my commitments? Who? What commitments am I willing to make?

_____

_____

_____

_____

Repeated Forgiveness *Romans 5:3-5*

1. Do certain behaviors and character defects that show up in my Step Ten inventory point to a pattern? Which ones? What is being revealed?

_____

_____

_____

_____

2. Am I having trouble admitting these properly in forgiving myself?

_____

_____

_____

_____

_____

3. Do I give myself grace? Why or why not?

_____

_____

_____

_____

_____

Be Angry and Don't Sin _Ephesians 4:26-27_

1. How have I experienced anger in my grieving?

_____

_____

_____

_____

2. What is my first response when I am angry?

_____

_____

_____

_____

3. How is anger dealt with in my family? By my mother? By my father? Which pattern do I follow?

_____

_____

_____

_____

4. When I am angry, can I promptly admit it? Why or why not?

_____

_____

_____

_____

5. Do I have support people who can help me learn to deal with anger more appropriately? Do I have someone I can talk with about my anger in my grieving? Am I willing to ask for help?

_____

_____

_____

_____

Spiritually Fit _1 Timothy 4:7-8_

1. Since this continual inventory is important for spiritual fitness, where in my daily routine can I set aside time to make self-assessment part of every day?

_____

_____

_____

_____

2. Do I have any resistance to evaluating my defects daily? What are my objections?

_____

_____

_____

_____

3. Here's an example of a simple, daily, personal inventory: Where have I been selfish, dishonest, fearful, or inconsiderate?

What have I done right today?

What do I need God's help with tomorrow?

What am I grateful for today?

Looking in the Mirror *James 1:24-25*

1. Have I been quick to recognize but not to take action in a particular area of my life or a defect of character? If so, can I take action without self-criticism by going back through Steps Six through Nine to work on that particular area or defect?

_____

_____

_____

2. In what area or in what defect do I need to take action today? This week? This month?

_____

_____

_____

Recurrent Sins *1 John 1:8-10*

1. Have I hoped for immediate release from my defects? Have I personally or unknowingly hoped that by doing all the step work I could attain perfection? Write any thoughts and feelings that arise from reading this meditation.

---

2. Is it clear that I still need inventories to continue my spiritual growth? Explain.

---

3. Do I sense that my conscience is returning or developing so that I may always more easily recognize my faults? Am I humble enough to admit that more readily? Record any progress.

Our lives require an ongoing evaluation of
our thoughts, deeds, desires, and motives.

PROFILE

Bob and Andrea were in leadership positions in an independent youth ministry. Their ministry had a powerful impact on their community and, consequently, a powerful impact on several local churches. The pastors in the area had great respect for Bob and Andrea's ministry and for their effectiveness. Their family was well-known and beloved.

They had two sons who were as different as any two brothers could possibly be. Andrew was a senior in high school, where he had been the top athlete in the school, playing and excelling in three sports. His younger brother, Peter, was an excellent musician. He couldn't care less about sports. For Peter it was all about music and worship.

Andrew had been recruited by a number of major universities, primarily for his football prowess. He had decided to attend the major university in their hometown. His high school was excited, and his family was equally excited. But the excitement soon came to a sudden halt when Andrew was diagnosed with a severe brain injury.

Andrew had suffered a concussion while playing football, but no one had realized it, and it was left undiagnosed. A few weeks later, Andrew suffered another concussion. This time it was caught, but it was too late, and the damage had already been done. Bob and Andrea got second, third, and fourth opinions from neurologists, but they all agreed that Andrew's condition was probably going to be permanent. The damage to his brain left Andrew as if he were a boxer who'd been knocked out too many times. He wasn't all there. He couldn't function on a team, so he couldn't play any of his sports. It was even unlikely that he would be able to attend college.

Bob and Andrea were Andrew's biggest fans, and they were crushed. Everything had to be put on hold. Each of the neurologists had said it probably would be a lifetime condition, but they didn't go into any further detail about what Andrew's life would be like. They all knew that they had to grieve losing their dream of Andrew becoming a football star at the local university. But beyond that, they didn't know what the additional losses might be, so they had no idea what else they were going to have to grieve in the days ahead. Apart from a miracle, grief was going to be a way of life for this family.

STEP ELEVEN

We sought through prayer and meditation to improve our conscious contact with God, praying only for knowledge of his will for us and the power to carry that out.

Step Eleven is the next review step, in which we practice a new way of living and a new way of praying and meditating. It is a review of the first three steps in our journey. Those beginning steps had to do with getting our relationship right with Jesus Christ as our Higher Power and surrendering our lives to him. Steps Four through Nine helped us search our hearts and lives, make confession, and try to make restitution as best we could. In Step Ten, we began the process of reviewing our lives on a regular basis to keep ourselves on track. Step Eleven gives us our marching orders as we seek "through prayer and meditation to improve our conscious contact with God."

If we look back at our prayers, we often discover that they consist mainly of our asking God to deliver something we want. "Give me . . . forgive me . . . bless me . . . fix me . . . show me . . . protect me" about sums up the content of most of our prayers. We connect with God in order to get things from him for ourselves or for someone else. We forget about the source and become fixated on the results that he gives. Step Eleven invites us to move beyond our self-centered motivations into a godly desire to know God better and understand what he wants us to do with our lives.

As in every step, some keywords make a huge difference. The first significant word is *sought*: "we sought . . . to improve our conscious contact with God." A relationship with God doesn't just happen. We must desire it, seek it, pursue it. Jesus promised that "Everyone who asks, receives. Everyone who seeks, finds. And to everyone who knocks, the door will be opened" (Luke 11:10). King David expresses this desire by praying, "The one thing I ask of the LORD—the thing I seek most—is to live in the house of the LORD all the days of my life, delighting in the LORD's perfections and meditating in his Temple" (Psalm 27:4). These are the words of a man seeking to improve his conscious contact with God.

Of course you will want to work this step through your grieving process. We want to get God's perspective on what we are grieving. All too often we get stuck in our own perspective, get frustrated with God, and feel like he has abandoned us. To move quickly through this stage of grief, it's important that this step become a way of life for us. Would our grieving process be different if we had been following this step before we lost our loved one? Would our grieving process be different if in the midst of our grieving we followed this step?

We can usually connect with God best when we have a place to step away from the hustle and bustle of life where we can commune with him privately in prayer. Yes, we can ask for things. But we also want to be sure to thank him, praise him, and wait quietly before him to allow him to light up our hearts, minds, and spirits. If we are having difficulty praying, we can use God's Word as a source of our prayers.

In some of Paul's letters to the churches, he includes written prayers for them. We can also pray these prayers for ourselves (see Ephesians 1:15-23, 2:16-21; Philippians 1:3-11; Colossians 1:9-14).

We can pray the psalms as if they were coming from our own hearts. In a number of his psalms, David shows his struggles with his relationship with God. Note that David often complains in the first half of the psalm, but then he affirms his relationship with God in the last part of the song. It's a great model to follow.

What about meditation? The model for meditation is found also in the Psalms: "I have hidden your word in my heart, that I might not sin against you" (Psalm 119:11). Hiding God's Word in our hearts is a form of meditation. The only other example of someone hiding God's Word in her heart is found in Mary, who hid the words of the shepherds about Jesus in her heart and then "thought about them often" (Luke 2:19). Another translation says she "pondered them in her heart" (Luke 2:19, NIV).

This step also directs us to pray for only two things. First, we must pray for the knowledge of God's will for us. In fact the step says to pray "*only* for knowledge of his will for us." The focus is on the here and now. Rather than asking God to fulfill our requests, we relinquish control of our lives to him. The shift makes God the focus, not us. His will is the purpose, direction, and the "why" of our lives.

The second thing we are to pray for is the power to carry out God's will in our lives. The prophet Isaiah reminds us that God is the source of our strength: "Those who trust in the LORD will find new strength. They will soar high on wings like eagles. They will run and not grow weary. They will walk and not faint" (Isaiah 40:31). We all struggle with impatience. Now we must learn to wait upon the Lord if we want to find new strength, especially when we are grieving.

Jeremiah also reminds us of a truth that he realized in the midst of his own grief: "The LORD is good to those who depend on him, to those who search for him" (Lamentations 3:25). It's important that we remember that God favors us, he is good to us, and he blesses us when we depend on him and when we search for him, which is an ongoing process. We can never get too much of God. We must never stop searching for all of his dimensions. Our challenge is to continue in prayer and meditation so that we grow closer to God and know more about his purpose for our lives.

QUESTIONS FOR **STEP ELEVEN**

Thirst for God *Psalm 27:1-6*

1. What am I seeking most from God?

_____

_____

_____

_____

2. What is most difficult about trusting God with my requests?

_____

_____

_____

_____

3. How do I pray for something that might not happen?

_____

_____

_____

_____

Joy in God's Presence *Psalm 65:1-4*

1. What keeps me from accepting and experiencing God's comfort?

_____

_____

_____

_____

2. What scares me about the probability that God wants to redeem my loss in some way?

_____

_____

_____

_____

Finding God *Psalm 105:1-9*

1. Is my grief changing from day to day? Am I moving through the process? Identify some ways that things are changing.

_____

_____

_____

_____

2. Am I becoming more aware of others' feelings and needs? What have I noticed today?

_____

_____

_____

_____

3. Make a list of what you can thank God for today.

_____

_____

_____

_____

Powerful Secrets _Psalm 119:1-11; Luke 2:16-20_

1. What Scriptures have I hidden in my heart in the midst of my grieving?

_____

_____

_____

_____

2. Meditation means to ponder Scripture throughout the day. What has been easy about meditation? What has been difficult?

_____

_____

_____

_____

3. Has meditation helped me in my grieving? How?

_____

_____

_____

_____

Patient Waiting *Isaiah 40:28-31*

1. How does impatience show itself in my grieving? In my relationship with God?

_____

_____

_____

_____

2. Am I impatient about my progress in grieving? Do I expect perfection?

_____

_____

_____

_____

3. Why is it hard for me to trust in the Lord?

_____

_____

_____

_____

God Is for Me *Job 19:8-27*

1. In my grieving or in working the steps, has God seemed like my enemy? In what ways?

_____

_____

_____

_____

2. Am I tempted to do God's will in my own power? In what situations?

_____

_____

_____

_____

God is on our side,
even if we can't see it now.

PROFILE

Jane was a single mom with a thirty-year-old son, Thomas. He had some problems with drugs earlier in his life, but for the past three years, he had been clean and sober. When he injured his shoulder and broke his collarbone, he was in great pain. The doctor had prescribed a strong opioid for him. Right after his injury he moved in with his mother because he knew he was in for a long rehab. Jane was nervous with the prescription around, but she kept an eye on it, and everything seemed to be okay.

Eventually Jane took Thomas to see the doctor for an evaluation prior to his surgery. He seemed agitated after the appointment, but he said he didn't need anything. Then he asked his mom for money so he could go out and get a hamburger. She gave him the money, and Thomas left, but he never came back home.

Jane was still up nervously waiting for Thomas to come home when two policemen came to her front door. She knew something terrible had happened. One of the policemen told her that her son had died, apparently from an overdose. They were kind and offered to give her any help, but she assured them she would be okay.

She found out later that Thomas was agitated after the doctor's appointment because he had asked the doctor for more pain medication. Instead he was given a prescription for a milder form of opioid, the opposite of what Thomas had requested. When the toxicology report was finished, it was determined that Thomas had died of an overdose of heroin and fentanyl, a deadly opioid when mixed with other substances.

He apparently didn't want a hamburger. He apparently needed something he thought would stop the pain.

After the policemen left, Jane sat there in stunned silence. All she could think of was that Thomas had died using her money. She had enabled him in his death. She was racked with so much guilt and shame that she could barely breathe, let alone grieve. Finally she called her best friend and told her how Thomas had died. Her friend came to her house immediately and stayed the night. She had to keep reassuring Jane that she was not responsible for his death simply because she gave him money. Finally Jane stopped blaming herself, and she began to grieve the loss of her son. She could not have done it without her friend's help.

STEP TWELVE

Having had a spiritual awakening as a result of these steps, we tried to carry this message to others and to practice these principles in all our affairs.

This step has three parts: First we need to have had a spiritual awakening; then we are to carry this message to others; finally we are to practice these principles in all of our affairs.

Let's look at the first part of this step—*having had a spiritual awakening.* The Twelve Step recovery program is often called a selfish program, and in some ways it is. It has to be if we are going to change. But those who work the first eleven steps find that when they come to Step Twelve, they have had a spiritual awakening. So it begins as a selfish program, but it becomes a spiritual program.

As soon as we find recovery, we want to share it with others. It's normal to want others to experience what we are experiencing. But we must temper that zeal realistically. It is too tempting to want to carry the message to others before we have lived the message ourselves. That's the reason this is reserved for Step Twelve. We don't begin recovery with Step Twelve; it comes after we work the first eleven. We work the steps this way so that we don't become instant authorities on something we haven't really experienced yet. If you haven't worked all the steps, you need to stop working on this step and go back to where you left off.

What does *spiritual awakening* mean? It is both a mystery and a miracle at the same time. A spiritual awakening could mean that over a period of time I begin to see God's hand in all that has happened. Connecting, praying, working the steps through the pain, and accepting the struggle as part of the process often draws a person closer to God and provides a spiritual awakening. Sometimes it's quick; other times it progresses slowly.

There is also a danger in thinking about a spiritual awakening as an event rather than a process. We may become discouraged if we do not experience a major or sudden shift in our emotions or thinking. But if we are open to the spiritual things of God, looking for God's hand in all that happens to us, moving toward God and not away from him, then we can be confident that we have begun the spiritual awakening. And when we are spiritually awake, we realize that others are not. This brings us to the second part of Step Twelve: *We tried to carry this message to others.*

Here is a story to illustrate this point: Once a man fell into a hole and began screaming for help to get out. A physician passed by and yelled into the hole that if the man could find a way out, he should come by the clinic and have his injuries treated. A lawyer came by and informed the man that he had a good case for a lawsuit, and if he ever got out of the hole, he should be sure to come by his office. The third man heard the cries, realized they came from his friend, and so he jumped down into the hole with him. The man who had fallen in could not believe it. He told his friend he needed help getting out, not someone to jump into the hole with him. The friend replied, "Don't worry: I jumped down on purpose. I've fallen in the same hole myself, and I know how to get out." He then told the man to follow him, and he led them out of the dark hole.

This is what we need and what we need to do for others. We need help from those who have been in the dark hole where we find ourselves. And once we get out, we need to be willing to jump back into the hole so we can help others find a way out. When we have been healed, it is our turn to carry the message of hope to others. The apostle Paul said, "If another believer is overcome by some sin, you who are godly should gently and humbly help that person back onto the right path" (Galatians 6:1).

The third part of this step is *practicing these principles in all our affairs*. It's not easy, but it sums up a life of recovery. To practice the principles found in the Twelve Steps in all our affairs produces a life of serenity, purpose, and meaning. It creates a manageable lifestyle in which we find ourselves connected to God in a new and intimate way. And we are drawn to others like never before. Let's review the principles:

> **Step One:** We must recognize our powerlessness in the unmanageability of our lives daily.
>
> **Step Two:** God removes our insanity and restores our wholeness.
>
> **Step Three:** We surrender to God and let go of control.
>
> **Steps Four and Five:** We make an honest inventory of ourselves (not others) and share our confession with another person. We also create and share our "new normal you" inventory.
>
> **Steps Six and Seven:** In humility, we seek help from God to cleanse us and fill us with new strengths.
>
> **Steps Eight and Nine:** We recognize the harm we have caused to others and take action to heal our damaged relationships.
>
> **Step Ten:** We continue to take inventory of our behavior, and when we are wrong, we promptly admit it.
>
> **Step Eleven:** We are increasingly more conscious of God's presence.
>
> **Step Twelve:** We give away what we have gained in our journey through the steps and remain in recovery in every life situation.

Practicing these principles is similar to what Jesus told his disciples: "Those who remain in me, and I in them, will produce much fruit. For apart from me you can do nothing" (John 15:5). We cannot practice the principles of the Twelve Steps without being connected to Jesus. Our priority is to apply the steps in any problem, event, situation, job, relationship, or loss—in other words, in anything that life brings to us—through the power of Jesus. When we connect to Jesus by deepening our conscious contact, he enables us to live more effectively, responsibly, and joyously.

Our shortsighted purposes for our lives begin to fade as we realize that with God's help we can conquer anything, even the task of grieving. The miracle of this partnership with God is so awe-inspiring that we are encouraged to continue recovery no matter how arduous it may be. We realize that material, worldly success pales in comparison to living vitally and purposefully. The book titled *Twelve Steps and Twelve Traditions* of Alcoholics Anonymous states, "True ambition is not what we thought it was. True ambition is the deep desire to live usefully and walk humbly under the grace of God."*

---

* *Twelve Steps and Twelve Traditions*, (New York, NY: Alcoholics Anonymous Publishing, 1986), 124–125.

QUESTIONS FOR **STEP TWELVE**

Our Mission *Isaiah 61:1-3*

1. How have I progressed through the pain and despair of my grieving? How close am I to healing?

_____

_____

_____

2. Having had a "spiritual awakening" in the grieving process, how can I share my experience with others?

_____

_____

_____

Our Story _Mark 16:14-18_

Write the story of your spiritual awakening and how your grief process contributed to the awakening. Describe how you have changed.

_____

_____

_____

_____

_____

_____

_____

_____

_____

Sharing Together _John 15:5-15_

1. Am I connected to the vine? How do the Twelve Steps help me to abide in him? Have I felt connected to the vine throughout my grieving?

_____

_____

_____

2. How have the changes brought about by working the Twelve Steps in my grieving process made me more loving towards others?

_____

_____

_____

3. What am I doing to reach out to others with Jesus' love?

_____

_____

_____

_____

Listening First *Acts 8:28-40*

1. What is my attitude about sharing my story of recovery? Am I reluctant to tell my story, or am I the kind of person who tends to share too much too soon with too many people?

_____

_____

_____

_____

2. Am I willing to wait for God's timing for sharing my story?

_____

_____

_____

_____

3. Do I see my story of grief or recovery as valuable to God's plan for me? Describe how.

_____

_____

_____

_____

Seeing Your Progress 1 Timothy 4:14-16

Paul encourages Timothy to "throw yourself into your tasks so that everyone will see your progress." What changes in my life might others observe since I have been grieving and working the Twelve Steps?

_____

_____

_____

Never Forget Titus 3:1-5

What memories do I have of what I've lost? Are they good memories? Describe some of the positive events that you want to remember.

_____

_____

_____

The Narrow Road 1 Peter 4:1-4

1. In what ways have I suffered physically for Christ in my grieving process?

_____

_____

_____

2. What do I still fear?

_____

_____

_____

3. How can I work the Twelve Steps regarding this fear?

_____

_____

_____

_____

CONCLUDING THOUGHTS

It has been our goal to help you with the grieving process. We hope this process has been beneficial. We also wanted to use the Twelve Steps as a guide through the grieving process. The temptation now is to think that we have finished the Twelve Steps, but the truth is that we never finish because we never quit growing emotionally and spiritually. We've taken you through a path and a process that, with God's help, can guide you through any problem you might face. That's why it's called Life Recovery.

You will carry this message to others as you integrate the principles into your daily living. You don't have to boldly proclaim this message; you just need to live it. The message is carried further and better by a kind tongue than by articulate lips. So carry a message of hope and transformation as you love others with all you have and all you are.

Here is a blessing that we hope will be an encouragement to you from the apostle Peter:

May God give you more and more grace and peace as you grow in your knowledge of God and Jesus our Lord. By his divine power, God has given us everything we need for living a godly life. We have received all of this by coming to know him, the one who called us to himself by means of his marvelous glory and excellence. And because of his glory and excellence, he has given us great and precious promises. These are the promises that enable you to share his divine nature and escape the world's corruption caused by human desires. In view of all this, make every effort to respond to God's promises. Supplement your faith with a generous provision of moral excellence, and moral excellence with knowledge, and knowledge with self-control, and self-control with patient endurance, and patient endurance with godliness, and godliness with brotherly affection, and brotherly affection with love for everyone. (2 Peter 1:2-7)

SCRIPTURE INDEX

Jeremiah 18:1-6 Giving Up Control
Lamentations 3:16-27 God Is Faithful
Ezekiel 33:10-16 Hope for Those Making Amends
Hosea 11:8-11 Covenant Love
Amos 7:7-8 The Plumb Line
Jonah 4:4-8 Going Deeper
Matthew 5:23-26 Peacemaking
Matthew 18:23-35 Forgiving Others, Forgiving Yourself
Mark 5:1-13 Internal Bondage
Mark 10:13-16 Like Little Children
Mark 16:14-18 Our Story
Luke 2:16-20 Powerful Secrets
Luke 8:43-48 Healing Faith
Luke 11:5-13 Pride Born of Hurt
Luke 18:10-14 A Humble Heart
Luke 19:1-10 The Blessing of Giving
John 5:1-15 Discovering Hope
John 15:5-15 Sharing Together
Acts 8:28-40 Listening First
Acts 17:22-28 Discovering God
Romans 1:18-20 Believe
Romans 5:3-11 Rejoice Always
Romans 5:3-5 Repeated Forgiveness
2 Corinthians 2:5-8 Grace-Filled Living
2 Corinthians 4:7-10 The Paradox of Powerlessness
2 Corinthians 7:8-11 Constructive Sorrow
Ephesians 4:26-27 Be Angry and Don't Sin
Philippians 2:5-9 An Open Book
Philippians 3:12-14 Attitudes and Actions
1 Timothy 4:7-8 Spiritually Fit
1 Timothy 4:14-16 Seeing Your Progress
Titus 3:1-5 Never Forget
Philemon 1:13-16 Unfinished Business
Hebrews 11:1-10 Hope in Faith
James 1:2-4 Rejoice Always
James 1:24-25 Looking in the Mirror
1 Peter 2:18-25 The Servant's Heart
1 Peter 4:1-4 The Narrow Road
1 John 1:8-10 Recurrent Sins
1 John 5:1-15 Unending Love
Revelation 20:11-15 God's Mercy